Marguerite M. Grueter

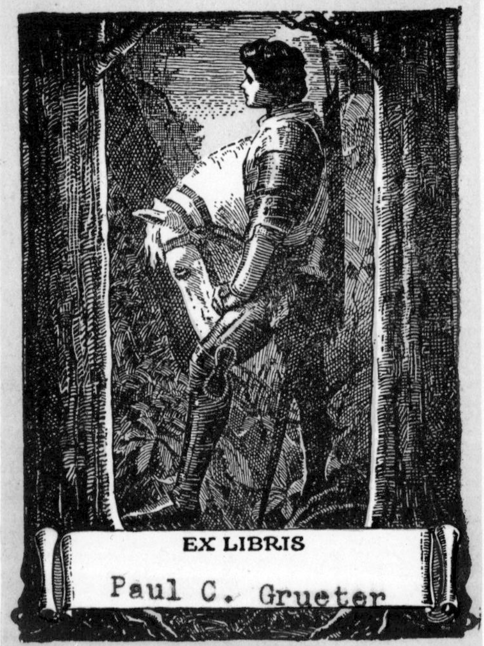
EX LIBRIS
Paul C. Grueter

COMPLETE CHEERFUL CHERUB

1001 VERSES

BY REBECCA McCANN

WITH A MEMOIR BY

MARY GRAHAM BONNER

CROWN PUBLISHERS
NEW YORK

PRINTED IN THE UNITED
STATES OF AMERICA

SECOND PRINTING, AUGUST, 1933.
THIRD PRINTING, MAY, 1934.
FOURTH PRINTING, MAY, 1935.
FIFTH PRINTING, APRIL, 1936.
SIXTH PRINTING, AUGUST, 1937.
SEVENTH PRINTING, DECEMBER, 1938.
EIGHTH PRINTING, 1939.
NINTH PRINTING, 1941.
TENTH PRINTING, 1942.
ELEVENTH PRINTING, 1943.
TWELFTH PRINTING, 1943.
THIRTEENTH PRINTING, 1944.
FOURTEENTH PRINTING, 1944.
FIFTEENTH PRINTING, 1945.
SIXTEENTH PRINTING. 1945.
SEVENTEENTH PRINTING, 1946.

MEMORIES OF REBECCA McCANN

IT SEEMS as though there had never been a time when I did not know Rebecca McCann, and now that almost five years have gone since pneumonia with unreasoning and swift cruelty took her away, only the permanent ache that remains makes one realize that she will not trip gaily into town from Chicago, Washington, the west coast, Europe, or any of the many parts of the world that saw her at some time or other.

She seems present not only because of her tremendous vividness and significance, but because of little things. I can see her so clearly with drawing board poised before her creating the Cherubs—her expressive small hands turning out with such sure, quick skill the work of her fertile and beautifully original brain. I speak of her beautiful originality because it was so natural. There are so many authors, artists, and intellectuals who make such a straining effort to be original, to refrain from being trite, and who, in their very effort to be different, are exceedingly commonplace. But not so Rebecca McCann. She thought originally—perhaps I could almost say that she felt with originality. There were no stereotyped emotions for her, and yet she was so human. And she seems so much with us now that when her sister and I talk, reminisce, we find ourselves drifting into the present tense about Becky—knowing so well what would annoy her, please her; small trifling things that would interest her—and then of a sudden the terrible realization that she is not here comes over us and we remember that a pitiful little handful of ashes were scattered over a lake in one of Chicago's parks—just as she had wanted it to be when the time came.

But the time came so wickedly soon—just as her hard work was beginning to bring returns, just as her diversified talents were generally appreciated, just as she was happy in her marriage—and she had had so much unhappiness.

Yes, I feel as though I had always known her. She talked to me so much about her childhood, I have heard so much from her sister and mother. So let us go back to the beginning, thirty years before that fatal one in 1927.

Rebecca McCann was born in Quincy, Illinois, where she spent the first few years of her childhood. On her father's side her ancestry was French and Irish and on her mother's side English. It was in Quincy that Frederic J. Haskin was a neighbor and he confirmed her mother's opinion that this wee girl was more than the so-called precocious child. Later when she grew up she worked for awhile for the Haskin newspaper service in Washington, interviewing people, writing stories, drawing pictures.

But before she could walk she could talk and she walked before any of the other children of her age could accomplish this youthful feat, strolling under the grand piano as her favorite sauntering route. Before she was two she was taken on her first trip to Chicago and had a small vocabulary of her own with which to point out what interested her. When she attained the age of two she went to kindergarten in Quincy and showed the characteristics which were hers throughout her life—a keen, absorbed interest in every flower, animal and person around her, a glorious capacity for enjoyment and just as great a sensitiveness to pain and cruelty. I can see her, as her mother tells me about those days, stamping her feet in uncontrolled rage because a horse was being beaten or a child corporally reproved, because I have seen her do just those very things in the streets of New York—this little, mild, quiet-voiced Becky with her tinkling, rippling laugh. Yes, often I have seen her suddenly stop and march into the midst of any fray where there was a question of cruelty.

During the first few years of her life Becky was telling stories to a group of children in the neighborhood—most of them older than herself. She had a sense of the dramatic and a sense of technique. She made her audience clamor for continuance—but did not yield until the time for the next installment.

Becky's first literary work was a story about a rabbit written at the age of six and published in the local newspaper. The rabbit died at the end of her story. There was always that awareness of sadness, even when she was a child, lurking about in all too neighborly a fashion.

But not only did Becky tell stories. She listened to those told to her by her grandmother, Amy Brett. I have always felt I knew that grandmother and that Becky was something like her. Amy Brett made everything interesting. She, too, was always flitting about the country and whenever she was away Becky wrote to her daily because her grandmother had once said that she hated to see the postman pass her door without stopping.

From Quincy, Mrs. McCann took her family to Peoria. Becky was always drawing in these days—drawing objects that had life, walking children, marching figures, leaping, swift-moving animals and flying birds. There was always movement in her work. Here she went to grammar school, and here, one day on returning home a waif dog followed her as she went through Bradley Park. She named the dog Bradley after the park, and when, later, two bull dogs killed him, Becky's rage and grief outdistanced the usual poignant sorrow a child suffers in the loss of a pet. Shortly after this her sister's canary "Admiral Dewey" died, and Becky began her first wonderings about the future life.

Injustice always enraged her. Her pleasure in her own pretty dress at a class celebration was changed to suffering because another little girl came in dull, drab garb.

After grammar school days were completed the family moved to Chicago. And here, as in Quincy and Peoria, all her teachers thought she was exceptionally clever. Algebra was the one subject she found difficult. She always carried a sketch book and a blank book, writing down thoughts which frequently became verses, and sketching people.

Becky attended the Englewood High School in Chicago and was valedictorian of her class when she was graduated. While here she won the scholarship of the Chicago Academy of Fine Arts which entitled her to instruction every Saturday afternoon. She also painted covers for sachets and began to save for a canoe, but it was hard to save for anything quite as large as a canoe and eventually the canoe became a hat. The family resources had diminished since the early days but throughout her youth Becky's mother gave her all the books she wanted, took her to concerts, gave her music lessons and fostered and appreciated her ability. In Chicago Becky had her own work room and drew pastel murals on the walls. While in high school it became necessary for Becky to earn money and she wrote and illustrated booklets for department shops, and wrote verses and painted pictures for the Volland Company.

After high school Becky attended the Chicago Academy of Fine Arts where she won another scholarship and remained another term. It was while she was here that one day she went to the offices of the Chicago *Evening Post* and saw Julian Mason, later the editor of the New York *Evening Post*. I remember her telling me about this some time afterward.

"I thought," she said, "that I would like to do some work

for one of the evening papers, so I went boldly to the newspaper office, carrying a large bag filled with samples of the work I meant to show. But in the excitement some odd little verses with drawings I hadn't meant to exhibit dropped out of the bag on the floor. He picked them up and looked at them carefully. I had made them only for my own amusement. I had written verses when I had gone out in the country for a rest a little while before. I had been nervous and tired. I had worked hard over my last year at school, and somehow everything seemed muddled and upset and tiresome. But out in the country the trees and the flowers and the butterflies and the clouds seemed so friendly. They gave me such nice restful thoughts that I began to show them I was grateful by writing them little thank-you notes. So I started writing the Cherubs and unexpectedly they were accepted and I began writing them as a daily feature."

That was the beginning of *The Cheerful Cherub.* It was Becky's title. But Mr. Mason's courteous picking up of the dropped pictures of a frightened seeker for work and his immediate appreciation and acceptance of them marked the beginning of a definite career. After this the Cherubs were syndicated and soon George Matthew Adams took them for his service and gave Becky the proper business management, coupled with loyal friendship.

Becky had no "mission" in life—perhaps that was why her verses meant so much to so many people. There was nothing patronizing about them. Human beings were always her equals.

"I'm not trying to reform the world or to make every one smile," she once told me in speaking about the Cherubs. "I'm trying to make my little verses human; they're sometimes sarcastic, sometimes they're 'flip'. They're cynical too, and I like to make them about all subjects—including the frailties of the readers—for their author understands frailties too!"

While she was doing the Cherubs for the syndicate she was also illustrating stories. I was fortunate in having her illustrate some of mine, and every bird, beast or insect had an individual touch, combining humor and expression of delectable variety. In addition to this she wrote a book "About Annabel" in which young Annabel encountered such entertaining companions as a Goojum bird, the Moon Man and the Pelican.

After she left Chicago and art school she went to Washington to work for awhile and then came to New York. It was war time and the world was tense and excited. It was during the last year of the war that Becky married a young aviator five days before he was to sail for the other side. His name was Harold Watson but he was always called "Jimmie." They both looked, and were, so young to be separated by such a paradoxically youthful misery as war. She took a very plain little house in a very lovely part of quite deserted country back of the Hudson River, but immediately it became a place of unusual charm. She couldn't stop overnight in an hotel—and she made many moves and fleeting trips in her life—that it didn't depart from its formal stiffness and quite naturally acquire a pleasing warmth of its own. I spent a few days with her in the little country house. She put up jam between writing and drawing Cherubs, planning for the return of her husband. On the neat little jars she pasted identifying labels and decorated them with cherubic faces possessing very wise and witty expressions, and flowery embellishments. In the evening we would get the water from the well and looking down into it pick out, in reflection, the stars we knew. And between times we would work. A katy-did talked loudly at night and by day became friendly enough to act as a model for a picture she drew.

Back to New York again after the flaming autumn had become subdued and settled, and there were long periods of waiting for letters, letters coming in batches—and then a longer wait than usual for letters. Then came the Armistice. But the wait for letters continued. It was a much longer wait than it should have been. It was. I was having tea with her one afternoon and she became almost hysterically nervous. She took out a little rough jacket of Jimmie's and put it on. She thought it would give her comfort as well as warmth and we heard a ring at the door. I suppose we had both been expecting that cable telling us that he had been killed. She spent most of her time with me that winter, going back to work in the day-time at her studio or at the offices of the syndicate where Mr. Adams felt it would be easier for her to have people working around her. Throughout the winter the letters came back—letters she had written to Jimmie and which had never been read.

Her second marriage to an officer in the Naval Medical Corps was unhappy and later she had to bring it to an end by divorce. But throughout all that happened to her a daily verse had to be written—and perhaps it was because she was not always so "cheerful" in her verses that she had so many different readers. After all, readers have their troubles and their sorrows and it meant something to them, as indicated by their letters, that some one understood. Her verses were so much a part of her life and not merely work that that was another one of the reasons that they were so distinctive. I can pick up her book and by reading the verses remember certain times in her life, happy or miserable, interested or worried, or of a concert we heard together, or a ride into the country.

Her last year was a joyous one and it pointed ahead to happiness. Her work was going well and her own life was serene. She married Harvey Fergusson, the novelist, in Galveston, Texas, and together they went to Salt Lake City. Harvey was working over a book with a southwestern setting and Becky's work could be done on mountain tops, hotel rooms, or sitting on a rock in a country field. Here they climbed mountains, swam, worked and mapped out their future with all the confidence that would have been realized had she lived, for they were supremely congenial and happy. They left here in December. They were going to spend Christmas with Harvey's family in

Albuquerque, New Mexico. He drove the car down in a snow storm, feeling it unwise for her to take such an arduous trip. She went to San Francisco to buy some clothes for the expected holiday gaieties, for she loved pretty clothes. She met Harvey in Albuquerque. But a slight cold turned into a heavy one as feverishly she gaily danced at a fancy dress party. She was ill only a few days. And then—

For the last time she went to Chicago.

MARY GRAHAM BONNER

New York City
June, 1932

GOOD OLD WORLD

I like the poor old
world, I do.
I sing its praise in
ode and sonnet—
It's strange it's not
a whole lot worse
With everybody
picking on it.

ABANDON

In winter I am stern
and strong.
My thoughts are cold
and high.
My intellect is
thawing now—
Three cheers for
spring, say I!

ABHORRENCE

Among the contraptions
My nature abhors
Are bookcases shaky,
With sticky glass
doors.

ACCEPTANCE

We live the most when
  we accept
Most fully what the
  days reveal,
For life is only, in
  itself,
An opportunity to
  feel.

ACCOLADE

Alone I want to go
  my ways.
I ask no help from
  anyone —
But oh, I want a lot
  of praise
For any work of mine
  well done.

ACCOMPANIMENT

Truth makes life a
noble thing,
And courage makes
it strong,
But grace and tact
must set them off
As music does
a song.

ACQUAINTANCE

I simply long to travel,
To visit every place,
And meet the various
members
Of the only human
race.

ACTING

If I go through the
motions of living
When sorrow has
deadened the heart of it
Life soon may seem
peaceful as ever,
For acting is
such a big
part of it.

ACTORS

My life which may
seem dull to most
To me is thrilling
every day —
We're all dramatic in
our minds
And live like
heroes in
a play.

ADJUSTMENT

To get adjusted to
the world
Is after all the
wisest aim.
It won't adjust itself
to us
For it was here
before
we came.

ADMIRATION

I welcome all my
friends' success
With loud applauding
cries —
But when they boast
and brag themselves
My admiration dies.

ADS

Among the ads in
 magazines
There lives a quaint
 and happy race,
Their problems solved
 by soap or soup,
A smile on every
 simple face.

ADVENTURE

I like to take a
 reckless step
Defying gaily all
 the fates —
Like plunging in an
 icy bath
It shocks
 but then it
 stimulates.

ADVENTURERS

Progress comes from
adventurers,
Explorers of land and
thought.
The absolute
conservative
Gives civilization
naught.

ADVERSITY

Though troubles help
to make us strong
Every time they
come,
I find it hard to
think of this
When I'm having
some.

ADVICE

At times you ought
to stay alone
I make so bold as to
advise
And just be friendly
with your soul—
Your soul will miss
you otherwise.

AFFECTATION

Whene'er I say
tomāto,
In syllables staccato
The proud and
haughty waitress
Repeats the word
tomato.

AFFLICTION

The members of our
  human race
Who move me most
  to scornful diction
Are sensitive and
  injured souls
Luxuriating in
  affliction.

AFFRONT

Although in doing
  worthy deeds
I've always quite
  exulted,
When told I had a
  good, kind heart
I felt somehow
  insulted!

AFRAID

Each life must have
some sorrow.
We cannot pick and
choose.
We never lose by
living—
By fleeing life
we lose.

AGE

Although old age is
creeping on
To all its troubles
I'm resigned.
My joints may stiffen
but I'll not
Have rheumatism in
my mind.

AIM

I do not aim for
wealth or fame.
I've other hope than
that —
I long to find before
I die
Just one
becoming
hat.

AIR

In gloomy moods it's
never wise
To sit at home and
mope.
Go out and take a
long brisk walk —
Fresh air creates
fresh hope.

AIR-FIENDS

I lie awake at dawn
  and think
How sad it is all over
  town
Lie other freezing
  souls like me
Who have to put the
  window down.

ALARM CLOCK

Although I'm wide awake
  at night
And counting sheep
  in numbers
When morning comes
  no power on earth
Can drag me from
  my slumbers.

ALAS!

I'd like to be most
tolerant
Of all that others do
and say,
The while I sternly
judge myself —
Alas, I'm just the
other way!

ALIEN

I feel a stranger on
this earth
Surprised at everything
I see —
I'm sure that somewhere
in the sky
Another world
was meant
for me.

ALOOF

The ancient sphynxes
calmly sit
Beneath the rain of
years—
So would I like to
take my life,
Unmoved by Time
or tears.

ALTARS

At dusk tall buildings
come to life.
Their windows glow,
now here, now there.
I feel their beauty in
my heart
As soft and
solemn as
a prayer.

ALTER EGO

I love to lie awake
at night
With not a thing to
hear or see.
That's when I get
acquainted with
The utter stranger
known as me.

AMBITION

I do not long for
wealth or fame.
I crave no laurel
wreath—
I yearn to turn a
handspring though,
And whistle
through my
teeth.

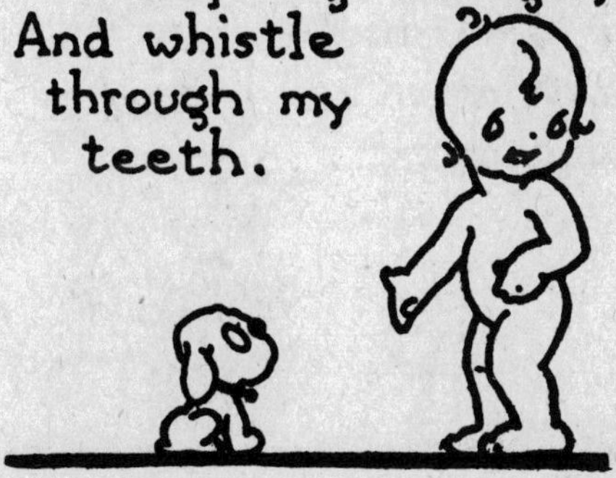

ANCESTORS

Posterity ought to be
grateful.
It's they whom our
battles are won for.
But ancestors cause
me more worry —
Poor things, they're the
ones that
are done for!

ANTIQUES

Antique furniture at
home
Wealth as well as
taste denotes —
Would that I could
start a fad
For wearing
antique
overcoats!

ANT-LIKE

I must reform my
ant-like mind
That carries small
stale crumbs of thought
And darts around
close to the ground,
Or paws the air
like one
distraught.

ANYWAY

I've had some awful
illnesses
And accidents that
stretched me flat,
But anyway I'm still
alive —
And lots of people
can't say that!

APOLOGY

If this cheerfulness
  annoys you
On the days you're
  feeling blue
Please forgive me,
  gentle reader—
Often it annoys me too.

APPARITION

I look into a mirror
And doubt reality—
A shadow of a
  shadow
My face looks back
  at me.

APPEARANCES

Misleading are
appearances.
One's true self is
within —
A corpulent outside
may hide
A soul that's starved
and thin.

APPETITE

My appetite for life is
large.
I want adventures
far away,
Yet leave untasted
half the time
The humbler
joys of
every day.

If the art of the
drama is poor
I'm a minor contributing
factor —
I clap at the worst
acts the most
I sympathize so with
the actor.

APPLICATION

Such grand and noble
thoughts on life
And how we ought to
live and grow
I write in great
profusion here —
It's harder to apply
them though.

APRIL

I love a day all green
  and grey
And musical with
  showers —
Along the ground there
  sweeps the sound
Of softly laughing
  flowers.

AREN'T WE ALL

True kindness just
  comes
From bearing in mind,
In our dealings with
  men,
That we're all of
  a kind.

ARGUMENT

I love a good hot
argument.
I'll talk for hours
anywhere—
But just one rule
must be observed:
To use statistics
isn't fair.

ARTISTS

We cannot all be
artists
Yet each one in his
place
Can give his daily
living
Artistic charm
and grace.

AS WE SEE OURSELVES ♀

We ask for under-
standing,
But often what we
mean
Is that all our
friends will see us
As we'd rather
we'd be seen.

ATLAS

Run away? Where will
you run to?
There's only this one
time-worn track.
The world isn't spread
out before you —
You carry your world
on your
back.

ATTENTION

I crowd the surface of
  my life
With all the things I
  do and see,
And so I'm lonely
  underneath —
I don't have time
  to notice me.

ATTIC CLEANING

We clean our houses
  every day
And throw the
  useless things away,
But often let our
  minds for years
Get filled
  with foolish
  thoughts
  and fears.

AT TWILIGHT

I love it at twilight
when violet dark
So softly envelops the
houses and park,
And the small frozen moon
pale with envy looks down
On the great
golden globes
that bloom
over the town.

AUDIENCE

It worries me when I
have talked,
Expanding views both
long and wise,
To see that hunted,
glassy look
Steal slowly o'er my
hearer's eyes.

AUTHOR! AUTHOR!

Friend Reader, if your
job is hard
Please pause and think
it might be worse—
At least when you are
feeling sad
You needn't write a
cheerful
verse.

AUTOBIOGRAPHY

In life my deeds have
been far from great
And my words have been
foolish and flat—
When I write my
autobiography though
I can easily change
all that.

AUTUMN

Youth and loves as
light as spray
Like fragrant petals
drift away.
Stark at last, and
somehow freed,
Stands the stalk
that bears
the seed.

AUTUMN WINDS

I love the wild cold
winds of fall
That blow the withered
leaves away,
Like storms in life
that free my mind
From old dead
thoughts of
yesterday.

AVERAGE

I want to live each
minute
With courage, zest
and grace,
Thus keeping up the
standard
Of the famous
human race.

AVIATION

I think I'll learn to
aviate—
There's so much traffic
everywhere
I'll simply let it have
the earth
And as for me—
I'll take
the air.

AWAKENING SPRING

Before we shed our
winter coats,
Before the last grey
snow departs,
A sudden thrill runs
round the world—
The spring comes
first in people's
hearts.

BABBLERS

Hundreds of people
paint pictures,
Hundreds write verses
like me —
Hundreds of brooklets
that babble
Are lost in the depths
of the sea!

BABIES

Babies reach for
anything
That's glittering to
see—
And though I'm old I
sometimes think
It's just the
same with
me.

BAD DEBTS

I can't abide people
who borrow from me
And never remember
the debt.
It isn't the principle
of the thing—
It's the money that
I regret.

BAFFLED

Life is most
mysterious,
But though it's hard
to see
A bit of reason for
it all
It means a lot
to me.

BALANCE

I can't regret my
many crimes
Though others view
them with alarm—
They've given me
experience
And thus done
good as well
as harm.

BARGAIN COUNTER

I rush to bargain
counters.
I will not be
impeded.
I find such wild strange
objects
I never knew
I needed.

BARGAINS

Life offers many
bargains.
It isn't those I
pray for —
The only things we
value
Are things
we really
pay for.

BARTER

I'd like to sample
other lives
And not keep on the
same old way.
Why can't we change
from time to time?
I'll trade, if
you will,
for a day.

BATHING SUITS

When pompous people
squelch me
With their regal
attributes
It cheers me to
imagine
How they'd look
in bathing
suits.

BATHTUB

How dear to my heart
is my flat in the city
When the home-coming taxi
presents it to view—
The farm of my childhood
is vineclad and pretty
But alas for
the bath tub
my infancy
knew!

BATTLING FATE

For all I know Fate
goes ahead
Its own ways, not
regarding us—
Well, if I cannot
change a thing
At least I'll
make an
awful fuss!

BEAUTY

Yes, beauty is more
than skin deep.
Sometimes glimpses
are caught
Of a beauty that lies
in the heart—
What a comforting
thought!

BEAUTY ETERNAL

Beauty is always
changing
To follow the changing
year,
Winter and spring
and summer—
Yet beauty is
always here.

BEES

I love it in the
country
But one thing
worries me —
The bees work all
day Sunday
Which really
shouldn't be.

BEST ANSWER

I hope that I'll
remember
When met by rude
invective
That silence is the
answer
That's always
most
effective.

BETRAYAL

I'm always caught in
telling fibs.
I have an honest
face, forsooth—
The while my heart is
black with lies
My simple
features tell
the truth!

BILLS

We have to pay for
everything.
Each reckless joy the
spirit wills
Goes past—and then
along comes life
Relentlessly collecting
bills.

BIRDS

Birds that perch on
fence and tree
Glance uncuriously
at me,
Not caring, as they
take my crumb,
Where I go,
or whence
I come.

BLESSINGS

They say our hardships
help us grow
And make us strong
and wise,
But if there's one
thing I dislike
It's blessings
in disguise.

BLISS

When I try to hold
my joy
It often turns to
woe,
For gladness, I should
realize
Must freely
come and go.

BLOSSOMS

The breeze goes
trailing carelessly
For miles along the
ground
A lovely, fragrant,
filmy scarf
It weaves of scent
and sound.

BOASTING

Although I envy people ease
It's strange that when I'm moved to boast
The many troubles I've endured
Are what I brag about the most.

BOOKS

The books I like the best are those
That give us more than what they say—
They simply open countless doors
Through which our thoughts can roam away.

BOREDOM

I wish I had a ticket
for Siam.
I'm getting pretty bored
with where I am—
But when I'm in Siam
why all I'll do
Is wish I had a ticket
for Peru.

BORES

Little idle stories,
Ancient jokes and
hoar,
Endless repetitions
Make the mighty
Bore.

BOUNTY

Money isn't worth a
 thing
Unless it helps the
 soul to live —
The richest man in all
 the world
Is he who has the
 most to
 give.

BOY SCOUT

To make my own life
 strong and free
Is really all I need
 to do —
Then where it touches
 other lives
It can't but make them
 stronger too.

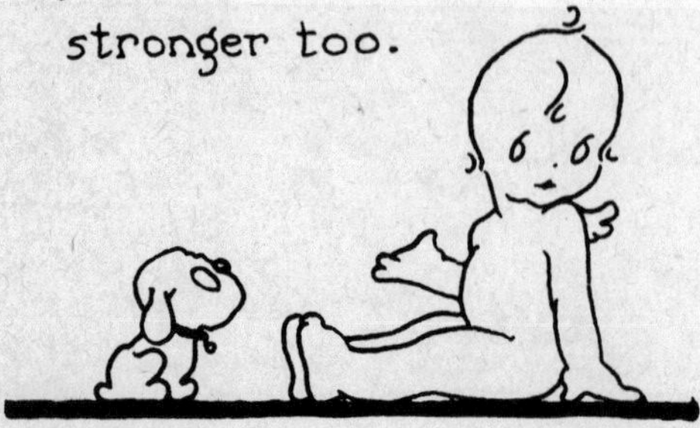

BRAGGARTS

When people loudly
  boast and brag
It always seems
  to me
They're trying to
  believe they are
The way they'd
  like to be.

BRASS BANDS

Beneath the vast and
  silent sky
The dauntless human
  race expands,
And celebrates its
  progress here
Triumphantly
  with loud
brass bands.

BRAVE HEARTS

Trust in life when
  sorrow comes
For life is like a
  current strong
That swiftly flows
  past little woes
And carries all
  brave hearts
  along.

BREAKFAST

The happy singing of
  the lark
Inspires many a poet's
  pen —
Let this then be a
  simple ode
To praise the
  good, hard-
working hen.

BREEZE

How sweet and brief
 the summer is!
She loves the world
 but never lingers —
I hold my hands up to
 the breeze
And feel the day run
 through
 my fingers.

BRIC-A-BRAC

The world is full of
 bric-a-brac
And things that
 gather dust —
No rest there'll be
 in life for me
If own such
 things
 I must.

BROADMINDED

I aim to have a kind,
broad mind
And yet, I must admit,
I find
That weaknesses I
most condone
Are always those
most like
my own.

BROKEN BUBBLE

Though we lose the first
joy of our youth,
That breaks like a
delicate bubble,
A stronger, more
durable joy
Comes after we've
weathered that
trouble.

BUBBLES

I think such grand and
noble thoughts
On how my life should
go —
Why is it when I try
them out
They always dwindle
so?

BUGS

I love the little
cheerful bugs
That chirp and sing
all summer long.
The summer days are
strung like beads
Upon their fine
unbroken song.

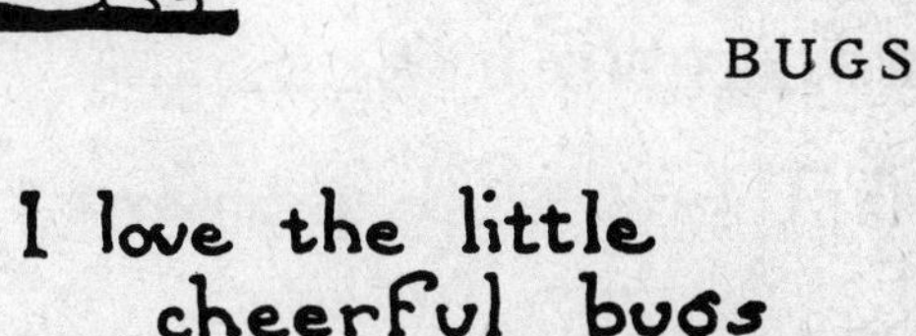

BUILDING ANEW

A sudden blow has
wrecked my world.
I'm disillusioned for
today.
But soon I'll build a
better one—
We make our own
worlds anyway.

BUILDING BLOCKS

I'll live each moment
to the full,
For though they soon
are gone,
Piled up they'll make
me quite a past
To build my
future on.

BURGLARS

A burglar stole my
jewelry
But that was really
kind—
No longer now my
jewelry
Can steal
my peace
of mind.

BUSY DIGITS

I sit and look at my
two hands
With sudden gratitude.
They work so willingly
for me
To earn my clothes
and food.

BUSY LIFE

Among the clothes and
calls and cards
That clutter up my
days
I feel I'm somehow
losing life —
I wonder if
it pays.

BUTTERFLY

The butterfly just
floats through life
As careless as a
bubble.
I walk a stern and
moral path —
A soul is
lots of
trouble.

BY-PRODUCT

Among my many long
dead loves
Which now look flat
and foolish
I prowl and poke for
things to write—
It seems a little
ghoulish.

CAKE

You cannot eat your
cake and have it.
So the cautious wise
ones wail.
But I shall eat mine
willy-nilly—
Otherwise it
might get
stale.

Quietly around the
earth
In golden sun and
rain and haze
Moves an endless
single file
Of lovely, many-colored
days.

CALLOUSED

Misfortunes used to
shock me so
I felt surprised at
every fall—
But now I've grown
so used to them
They hardly
bother me
at all.

CAMELS

I never think of
camels much,
But always see them,
when I do,
In endless caravans
although
I s'pose they have
their home
life too.

CAMOUFLAGE

Anger at another's
fault
I cannot honestly
condone —
It's nearly always
just a way
We turn attention
from our
own.

CARE

Courage can lessen
misfortune
To quite a surprising
degree—
The trouble is never
with trouble
So much as it is
with me.

CAREFREE

Never hurry, never
worry,
Live with leisure,
grace and care—
For it's plain that
constant rushing
Never gets you
anywhere.

CAROUSAL

I'm weary of serious
sensible souls.
Be jolly and silly,
say I —
For life should be gay on
a world that just rolls
Like a merry-go-round
through
the sky.

CAST-OFF

Let go of your
troubles.
Why cling to them
so?
They float off like
bubbles
When once
you let go.

So often we think of
such brilliant ideas
And then simply lose
them in space —
The air must be crowded
with wisdom unused
Cast off by this wise
human race.

CAT

I fuss and chatter
through the day.
I sew, I read a silly
book.
The cat who lies and
thinks for hours
Just gave me
one long
weary look.

CAUTION

Though caution is a
help I know
Don't let it be your
only guide
For when you watch
your step too much
You'll find it
rather cramps
your stride.

CELESTIAL HARMONY

The stars move in
their ordered ways.
All growing things
appear in season.
And I should try to
make my days
As neat as theirs
and ruled
by reason.

CERTAINTY

Though life is most
  uncertain
I'm sure of this one
  thing—
That when I'm in the
  bath tub
The telephone
  will ring.

CHANGE

If you feel you need
  a change
I know a simple
  thing to do—
Shut your eyes, then
  open them
And take a
  different
point of
  view.

CHANGING BEAUTIES

I feel I cannot love
 enough
The changing beauties
 of the year—
How wonderful my
 life might be
If worthy of
 its background
 here.

CHANGING ORDER

"Old times were best,"
 some people say,
Bewailing every
 modern ill,
Reproaching everyone
 because
The world will
 simply not
 stand still.

CHARACTER

I'm stern and high-
principled to a degree.
I never do things by
half measures.
Just one thing my
character can't do to me—
It can't interfere
with my
pleasures.

CHARGE ACCOUNT

I love to have a
charge account.
It makes for painless
buying—
Except that when the
bills come in
My family's so
trying.

CHARITY

My many mean and
  wicked deeds
At least have made
  me see
I surely should forgive
  the world
For what
  it does
to me.

CHARMS

All the world's a stage,
  they say,
That Fate's directing
  for us.
Some have starry
  parts to play
But I am in
  the chorus.

CHASE

I long for a life of
more leisure.
I rush through the day,
till it feels
As if I am chasing
tomorrow
While yesterday
snaps at
my heels.

CHATTER

The simplest social
call will bring
Engagements filling
time and space—
Oh, where on earth
can I escape
The always-talking
human
race!

CHEATED

To profit by another's
loss
Will, in the long run,
never pay—
I'd rather be the
cheated one
Than be the cheater,
any day.

CHECK BOOK

I cannot keep my
check book straight—
I find, to be quite
frank,
I'm much too lavish
with myself
And stingy with
the bank.

CHEERFUL CHERUB

Have you noticed,
Reader dear,
I am sometimes
gloomy here?
That's to give you
all a rest —
A constant smiler
is a pest.

CHEESE

Although for years
expensive cheese
In secret I have
hated
I eat it with
pretended ease
To seem sophisticated.

CHEF

Musicians win both
wealth and fame
With tremolos and
quavers —
Why are not cooks
immortalized
For symphonies
in flavors?

CHERRIBLE

I've been so cheerful
here so long
It's getting simply
terrible.
I think in verses all
the time —
My mind's turned
cheerful
cherrible!

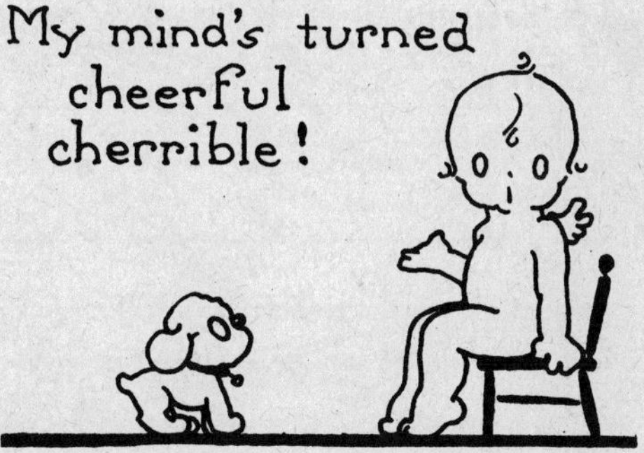

CHILDREN

Children in the city
street
Chirp and chatter
through the day,
Making through the
noise of work
The undercurrent of
their play.

CHIRPS

The earth is glad all
summer long—
It sings a never-ending
song,
With locusts, bees and
murmuring trees,
To which I add such
chirps as
these.

CHORES

The details of life
make a web —
My spirit would soar
free and high
But caught among work,
clothes and meals
I'm buzzing
around like
a fly.

CHRISTMAS BOXES

How lovely Christmas
boxes look,
All holly-trimmed and
ribbon-tied!
It's often quite a
shock to see
The funny things
there are
inside.

CHRISTMAS GREETINGS

Christmas wishes fly
like birds
Through the air on
Christmas day—
And mine, dear Reader,
fly to you
To wish more
joy than
I can say.

CHRISTMAS SHOPPING

Well, since I'm always
late with shopping
At last I've thought
of what to do—
This year I'll buy each
friend two presents
And label one
for next
year too.

CINDERS

The wind can blow a
house away
And lift the ocean
waves on high.
Why will it stoop to
little tricks
Like blowing
cinders
in my eye?

CIRCLES

The moon moves the
tide in the sea,
While the sun with its
strong golden light
Draws the human tide
out every day,
And then sends
it home
every night.

CIRCUMSTANCES

I live my life with
  self-respect,
Take credit for my
  lucky chances,
And when I fail I
  simply say
I blame it all on
  circumstances.

CITY NOISES

The noise of the city
  reaches high
But it fades at last
  in the quiet sky,
And the proud loud horns
  and the clanging cars
Are a faint soft
  murmur beneath
  the stars.

CITY SONG

The clamor of the
city
Seemed harsh and
loud and strong
Till I heard it from
a distance
And it made
a sort
of song.

CIVIC BEAUTY

Although the city hurts
my ears
With whistles, bells
and cries
There's always something
beautiful
On which
to rest
my eyes.

CLEVERNESS

Sometimes I feel a
little bored
By writers who are
merely clever
But when I spring
a clever thing
I simply cherish it
forever.

CLIMAX

I always kept thinking
when I was small
There would come one
climax greater than all,
But now, as plodding
through life I go,
I begin to
wonder if
this is so!

CLIMBING

To climb a mountain
to the sky
Is easier for me
Than struggling from
the way I am
To how I
want to be.

CLINGING

Only the weak will
try to cling
Too long to any
passing thing—
The strongest man is
he who stands
And lets life
run through
open hands.

I'd like to throw away
  the clocks
That chop to minutes
  all our days—
I'd rather tell the time
  by meals
Or sun or such-like
sweeping ways.

CLOTHES-HORSE

Although of course I
  buy my clothes
To cover up my
  fragile frame
The only thought I
  have in mind
Is how they'll
  decorate
  the same!

CLOUDS

Each kind heart is
like a sun
That shines upon the
passing crowd—
How sad I feel on
selfish days
When I have
lived behind
a cloud.

CLOWN

We learn from our
mistakes they say
And I'm a living proof
it's true—
Each year I'm nearer
perfect in
The wild and
foolish things
I do.

COLD SHOWER

Crown me with a hero's
wreath
Of every rarest
flower
For I arose this
freezing dawn
And took an
ice cold
shower.

COLDEST HEART

Spring spreads magic
through the world
With flowers and bird-
songs everywhere,
And even in the
coldest heart
She sometimes
plants a
love affair.

COMEDY

That we pursue our
solemn lives
Upon a rolling, spinning
earth
Seems such a funny
thought to me
I simply scream with
helpless mirth.

COMFORT

Three things I have
for perfect bliss,
No farther need I
look :
An open fire burning
bright,
An apple and
a book.

COMMON SENSE

Common sense is
good to have
But never let it
master you—
For then it might
deprive you of
The foolish
things it's
fun to do.

COMMUNION

Now the air is blue
and golden,
Shimmering and warm
with sun.
I can take deep
breaths of summer—
Sun and earth
and I
are one.

COMPANIONS

I wish my dog could
talk to me.
With thoughts his eyes
are big and dark.
How sociable our days
would be
If he could speak or
I could
bark!

COMPENSATION

Joy as well as woe
All of life composes—
If every rose has
thorns
At least most thorns
have roses.

COMPLAINTS

When I complain it
often means,
No matter how I rage
and whine,
I'm really blaming all
the world
For faults I
will not face
as mine.

COMPLIMENTS

No compliment that
I receive
Seems undeserved
to me —
I see myself, not
as I am
But as I
want
to be.

COMPROMISE

Some lives are thwarted
so by rules
They can't be glad
and free —
To make our rules suit
life instead
Seems wiser far
to me.

CONCERT

My hearts always soothed
by sweet music
When life seems quite
hopeless and bad.
It's not that it makes
me feel happy —
It makes me
enjoy feeling
sad.

CONDUCT

A rule for good
conduct
Which hasn't failed
yet
Is just to do
nothing
You'd like to forget.

CONFESSION

Although I'm often
foolish
And my life is full
of breaks
I make a sort of
virtue
Of admitting
my mistakes.

CONFIDENCE

It's not my many
foolish crimes
That fill me with
regret —
It's just that I've
confided them
To friends who can't
forget.

CONSCIENCE

Sometimes at night
my conscience wakes
With pangs it seems
that naught can lull.
If I could always
feel like this
How good I'd be,
and oh,
how dull!

CONSEQUENCES

It's foolish to regret
   mistakes
For everybody makes
   them—
The consequences matter
   not
As much as how one
   takes them.

CONSOLATION

Trouble cannot keep
   me down—
When life seems all
   a deep, dark blue
I know a little secret
   spring
Of joy will soon come
   chuckling
   through.

CONTENTMENT

Well, here I sit, a
little thing,
Contented in the sun,
And think how warm
and gay life is,
What though it soon
is done.

CONVENTION

I do not mind conventions
now.
I know just how to
take them—
I keep them till I'm
bored and then
Exultingly
I break
them.

CONVERSATION

Although to talk about
  myself
I always madly
  yearn
I'm not as bad as
  some— at least
I give my friends
  their turn.

COPY

People's faces tell us
  tales,
Strange and sad
  and funny—
My thoughts fly seeking
  them, as bees
Go flying after
  honey.

COQUETTE

Of course I never
really flirt.
It isn't ladylike I
know.
The way I drop my
handkerchief
Is simply
providential
though!

CORRESPONDENCE

The guilt of not
answering letters
Weighs down on my
conscience at night.
I suffer and groan in
the silence
But nothing can force
me to write.

CORROBORATION

The books I like to
read the best
Are always, if the
truth be told,
The ones that just
corroborate
The views that I
already hold.

COSTUME

I long to dress with
care and taste—
Alas, I always lose
my mind
And when I enter
any shop
I act both
wild and
color-blind!

COTTONWOOD

The breeze blows the
cottonwood tree
And its green leaves
turn silvery grey,
And somehow that turns
all my thoughts
From solemn
to twinkling
and gay.

COURAGE

If you have tried and
tried again
Nor made your effort
less
You really have
succeeded then—
For courage is
success.

COWARDICE

Although I'm brave
enough, I'm sure,
To meet life's gravest
situations
I lack the courage to
refuse
My dull friends' dinner
invitations.

COWARDLY ACTS

I never would lie to
a friend.
I carefully stick to
the facts —
Then why will I lie
to myself,
Excusing my cowardly
acts.

COWS

If I could only stand
and think
As placid as a cow
How much more simple
life would be
That's so distracting
now.

CRIMES

Of all the many crimes
My wicked past
bestrewing
I most regret
the ones
That some one
caught me
doing.

CRIMINAL

Though my acts at
times look wicked
I am sure that I'd
seem good
If my underlying
motives
Were completely
understood.

CROCUSES

Life sometimes seems
a barren field
That far and grey
around us spreads,
But unexpected little
joys
Like crocuses
thrust up
their heads.

CROWD

When I'm alone I'm just
 honestly me,
Not foolish or humble
 or proud.
But when I'm with others
 I'm acting a part—
I always
 get lost
 in a crowd.

CRUDITY

My crude baby sister
 makes terrible breaks,
And nothing we do seems
 to stop her.
She won't be unnatural,
 scold as we may—
And we all know that
 Nature's improper.

To read a book for
culture
I cannot keep
awake —
I never like the
classics
Excepting by
mistake.

CURE

I know a way to
cure the blues
As sure as anything:
Turn on the bath tub
water hard
And then get in and
sing.

CUT-AND-DRIED

I lift my voice in
long loud wails
When troubles come
to me
Yet take for granted
all my joys—
This really
shouldn't be.

CYNIC

The cynic says the
world's a sham,
That nothing's good or
true.
And does he then
include himself
In this broad
statement too?

DAILY TASKS

Unless I liked my
daily tasks
I'd feel a strong
misgiving
That though I did my
work to live
I wasn't really
living.

DARING

I like a life of
daring,
To make mistakes
and then
Look forward, never
caring,
And take
new risks
again.

DAY AFTER DAY

Like petals from the
  bloom of Time
The colored days
  float past.
And one by one they'll
  lightly come
And bury me
  at last.

DEBATE

I argue, argue constantly,
With countless words
  assert my will,
Yet anyone can
  baffle me
By calmly, wisely
  keeping still.

This day I devote
Each and every
December
In thinking of
friends
I forgot to
remember.

DECISION

Whenever a problem
comes up in my life
I decide it and
promptly forget it—
It isn't so much the
decision that counts
As the will power not
to regret it.

DEEDS

The past is represented
by
The things that we
accomplish in it,
And measured thus
whole months of mine
Seem now no longer
than a minute.

DEEP STUFF

Deep books by wise
philosophers
(I'd say it with my
final gasp)
Just tell of things I
always knew
In words I simply
cannot grasp.

DELICACY

Delicate things are
the truest things—
The lightest word or
thought or touch
Means more than loud
and heavy speech
That lies because it
says too
much.

DELUSION

Those who feel their
sorrows deeply
Feel their joys more
keenly too,
And thus they live all
life with fervor—
At least they like
to think
they do.

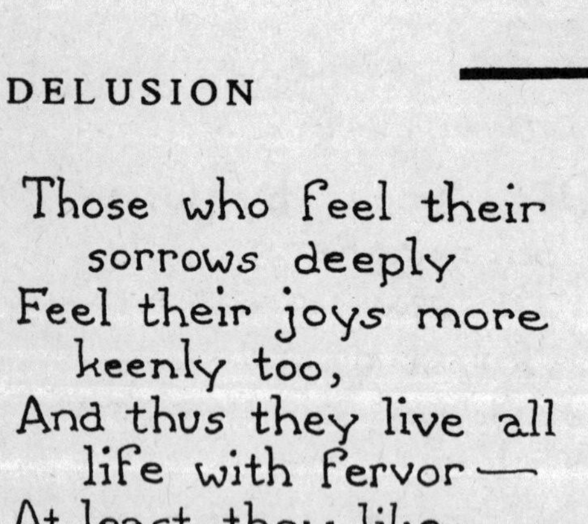

DEMANDS

To ask is not the
  way to get —
Alone and proud the
  strong man stands
And people give much
  more to him
Than to the
  weak who
  make demands.

DEMOCRACY

I feel my kinship
  with the low.
They're good as I am
  any day —
It irritates me
  quite a lot
To find that
  they too feel
  this way.

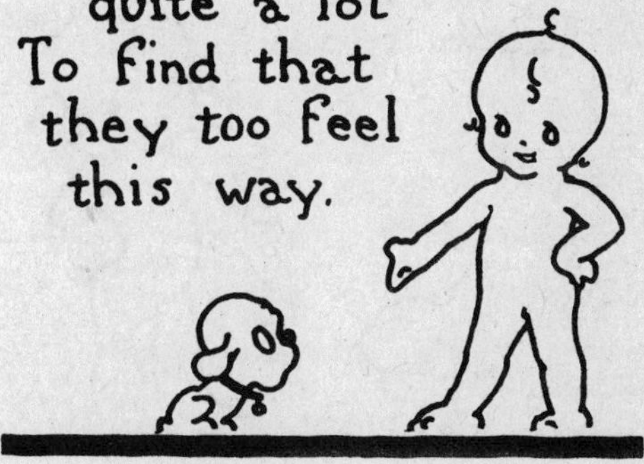

DEPTHS

Trouble never lasts
for long—
Although I wail and
agonize
When once I've reached
the depths of woe
I know I'll
soon begin
to rise.

DERISION

If I laugh at myself
And the fool things
I do
It won't bother me
much
To see others
laugh too.

DESIGN

I make the texture
of my life.
Of raw materials I
weave it.
And light and dark
will blend, I hope,
In harmony, before
I leave it.

DESIRES

Unless we can master
our own desires
They say we can
never be free—
A sensible thought and
a true one too,
But a little
annoying
to me.

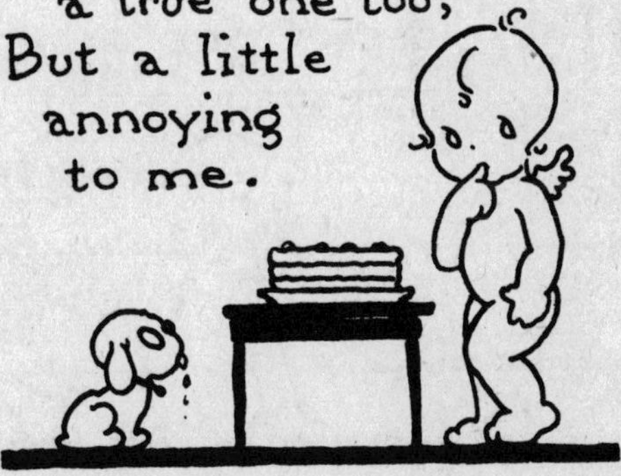

DESKS

I wish I had a row
of desks
Extending endlessly
away,
For then I'd never
clean them up—
I'd use a new one
every day.

DETACHMENT

A detached point of view
is a wonderful thing
For it doesn't detach one
from others.
The less I'm wrapped up
in my personal life
The closer I get to
my brother's.

DETAILS

I don't see life in
the abstract
As something sweeping
and grand—
I bury my head in
its details
As an ostrich
does in
the sand.

DETERMINATION

Although my way
seems hard
I'll waste no strength
in crying—
For no one ever
failed
Unless he
gave up
trying.

The humble part I play
in life
Does not much help my
self-esteem—
But in the diary I
keep
You'd be surprised
how grand
I seem.

DIFFICULTIES

My difficulties test
my strength
So, as I struggle
through,
By teaching me to
know myself
They really
help me too.

DIGNITY

I'd like to skip along
the street
But I must walk
with stately stride.
Who started all this
foolishness
Of people
acting
dignified?

DILEMMA

To run or not to run —
that is the question.
Whether 'tis better from
the tub to spring,
And race all dripping at
the 'phone's loud ringing,
Or just to sit and
let it ring
and ring.

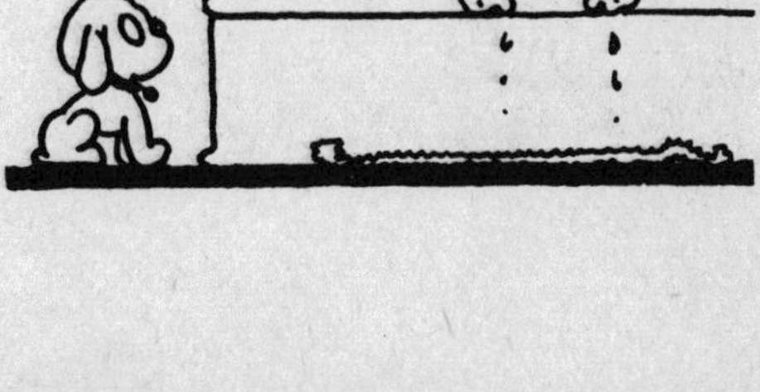

DINNER PARTY

When I'm giving a dinner
things often go wrong.
I'm far from perfection
as host.
At least I have never
apologized though—
Let this be my one
humble boast."

DIRECTING OTHERS

Those who freely give
advice
May do it not to help
alone—
Directing some one
else's life
They feel that
they enlarge
their own.

DISAGREEMENT

When a thoughtful eye
I cast
O'er my long
disastrous past
I must admit I
seldom see
My principles and
acts agree.

DISAPPOINTMENTS

A tree stands firm and
strong in fall
Though winds may strip
its leaves away—
Thus disappointments
strip my life
But strength
and hope can
always stay.

DISCONTENT

Contentment is a
priceless gift,
But discontent is
helpful too—
I want the first for
what I have,
The second, though,
for what
I do.

DISCOVERY

I found a way to
cure today
That foolish mood of
hurry—
I simply stopped the
clock and then
I didn't have
to worry.

DISCRETION

I'm honest as the day
is long,
But only through
discretion:
I cannot tell a lie—
I lack
Control of my
expression.

DISGRACE

I'd rather be the
lowly soul
Who suffers every
deep disgrace
Than wear that sly
rejoicing look
That sometimes lights
a righteous
face.

DISHWASHING

Today I broke another
plate —
It quite delights me
now and then
To think there's one
at any rate
I'll never
have to
wash again.

DISPLAY

I go to heavy
concerts
And study heavy
books
But not so much for
pleasure
As just for how
it looks.

DISTANCE

Although there's beauty
near at hand
To distant lands my
dreams all stray.
I see the loveliness
of home
Most clearly
when I'm
far away.

DOMESTIC

Hands of artists bring
us beauty,
Giving form and sound
to dreams —
Other hands enrich our
lives too,
Baking bread
and sewing
seams.

A door is so adaptable
It leads to spaces
wide,
Or when you want
to be alone
It shuts
the world
outside.

DOUBLE LOSS

On my way to the
dentist today
My very best hat
blew away
And, believe it or not
but it's true,
I then lost
the heel
off my shoe!

Though words may seem
to be direct
Their meaning often
is twofold —
When people say,
"How young you look!"
I realize
I'm getting
old.

DRAMA

I walk through my
days like an actor
Who dresses and
gestures a part,
And only at times show
the stranger
Who lonesomely
lives in my
heart.

DRAMATICS

I like to act a part,
So when I get a
blow
I never suffer
much
I dramatize it so.

DREAMS

Through my saddest,
blackest mood,
Small and very far
I see my future
happiness
Shining like
a star.

DRIFTING

I do not strive to
  guide my life
With firm and brain-
  restricted hand—
So often, drifting here
  and there,
I touch the
  shores of
  fairyland.

DULLNESS

If you call the world
  dull
You will maybe find
  out
It is really yourself
You are talking
  about.

DUMBNESS

Dumb animals we call
them
While they bark and
neigh and moo.
They talk as much
as we do—
To them we seem
dumb too.

DUST

I love the world—
when die I must
Beside a road I want
to lie
And feel upon my
grave the dust
Of life
forever
passing by.

DUTY

Now duty is a horrid
word.
Right-doing should
be glad—
If you do good
because you should
You might
as well
be bad.

EARLY BIRD

Hear the early birds
rejoicing—
How they twitter and
they sing!
While the early worm,
poor fellow,
Never says a single
thing.

ECONOMY

It's easy to save
By refraining from
giving
But a generous
heart
Makes us richer in
living.

EDUCATION

I sometimes wish my
dog could read
But if he could perhaps
he'd find
A lot of things to worry
him
That now have never
touched his
mind.

EFFICIENCY

I must be more
efficient
In the life that I've
designed —
I'm a careless
imitation
Of the self
I have
in mind.

EFFORT

My teachers criticise
me
And say I loaf and
shirk.
I'd do great things
to show them —
Except it's so much
work.

EGO

In all my thoughts
how big I seem!
I stand conspicuous
in space,
While, like a chorus
on the stage,
Behind me
stands the
human race.

EINSTEIN

When I relinquish
thoughts of wealth
And quit its blind and
futile chase,
Freed from possessing
little things,
I'll own instead
all time,
all space.

ELEMENTS

Lightning and thunder
I love
And winds that are
reckless and high—
Like a leaf is my
spirit whirled up
And away,
down the wide,
shouting sky.

EMANCIPATION

I sometimes try to
manage other people
Till suddenly I see
That only when we give
each other freedom
Can we ourselves
be free.

EMBROIDERY

Words embroider all
we do —
Playing, working,
walking,
We weave our lives
together with
The lacy sound
of talking.

EMINENCE

When the president
goes fishing
Do mosquitoes bite
him too
With no more
consideration
Than they have for
me or you?

EMPTINESS

The ones who seek
 their happiness
By buying cars and
 clothes and rings
Don't seem to know
 that empty lives
Are just as empty
 filled with
 things.

EMPTY HEAD

I'm trying to empty
 my mind
Of every thought
 foolish and small—
I wonder if then I
 shall find
There's anything
 left at all.

ENERGY

I feel so full of vim
today
My daily tasks I
shirk —
I can't waste all this
energy
On nothing
more than
work

ENNUI

The only times that
I am bored
And wearily complaining
Are those when I
myself, I find,
Am far from
entertaining.

ENVY

Nearly all that gossip
shows
Is that the gossips
envy those
Who dare to go their
own free way
And never fear
what others
say.

EPIGRAMS

I think of epigrams
at night—
Next day I start
long conversations
And work for hours to
get a chance
To show my friends my
scintillations.

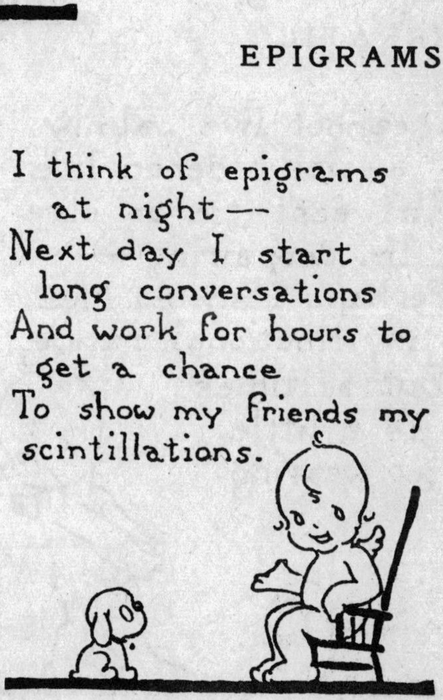

EQUALITY

Of course we're free
and equal here
In spite of fame or
pelf.
Some seem more free
than others though—
I'm "equaller"
myself.

ERRATIC

I cannot live calmly
a well-ordered life.
I'm ecstatic or else
I'm despairing—
Perhaps I should like
my emotional range
But at times
it's a little
bit wearing.

ESCAPE

The letters and the
 calls I owe
Have filled me so
 with shame
To some far land
 I'll have to go
And hide
 and change
 my name.

ESTHETE

I sit beneath a
 broiling sun
And, sore beset by
 ant and bee,
A martyr to the cause
 of art,
Laboriously I draw
 a tree.

ESTRANGED

I watch my little
dog asleep—
It certainly seems
queer
How strange and distant
sleep can make
Even the one most
dear.

ETERNAL YOUTH

Time just affects the
physical—
Old age they need not
fear
Whose minds grow more
adventurous
And younger
every year.

ETERNITY

Waves rise and fall—
while on the shore
In slower rhythm
flows
All life, that grows
and blooms and dies
And then, in new waves,
grows.

ETHICS

When questions sad
beset the mind
On what is false and
what is true
I find that work at
least is real—
It's good to
have a
job to do.

ETIQUETTE

I love hotels, complex
and vast.
Each year they're
grander than the last.
I wish they had
instructors though—
I miss a lot
of tricks
I know.

EVANESCENCE

A mood of gladness
comes and goes.
As lightly as a moth
it lingers.
But when I try to
grasp it close
It only dies
within my
fingers.

EVENING

The sun sets in a
flame of gold,
The pale moon casts a
lovely spell,
And sleep and rest the
world enfold—
I think these
things are
managed well.

EVOLUTION

To complain because
life isn't perfect
Seems captious and
petty of soul—
When you think the
world started with chaos
It did pretty well
on the whole.

EXAGGERATION

I cut my finger with
a knife.
I neither wept nor
moaned nor swooned.
In fact the courage
that I showed
Was worthy
of a larger
wound.

EXCEPTIONS

I try to be friends with
the whole human race
And feel they're my
brothers whatever they do,
Except those at concerts
who sit next to me
And put on their
rubbers before
it's all through.

EXCHANGE

Though some would
welcome gifts like these
To me they seem both
wild and strange—
It might be quite a
public boon
To start a
Christmas
Gift Exchange.

EXCUSES

I can always make
excuses
When I'm disinclined
to work
But when I am hiring
some one
How I hate to see
him shirk!

My road through life
is rough at times,
With hills that dip
and rise.
But this all helps my
character—
It needs the
exercise.

EXPECTATION

Standing on the edge
of time
I love to look ahead
and see
The rows of fresh new
days all filled
With strange
surprising
life for me.

EXPLOSION

"When everything goes
dead wrong"
And fate presses down
on my load,
Am I noble and brave?
No, I break things and
rave—
It's such
a relief
to explode.

EXTRAVAGANCE

I'm all for careful
saving—
I hoard for weeks my
cash
Because I love to
spend it
In a great,
big splash.

EYES

One thing when
 sorrow comes to me
Has helped my spirits
 rise —
The quiet courage
 that I see
In other people's
 eyes.

FACADE

My great lack of wisdom
 embarrassed me once
But at last I've acquired
 more guile —
When a subject comes up
 I know nothing about
I just smile a superior
 smile.

FACES

We'd find each face
was beautiful,
However plain it seems,
If, looking past the
dull outside,
We saw the wistful
dreams.

FACIAL

One spot I know where
sham and show
And posing have no
place —
And that's the beauty
parlor where
They renovate
my face.

FACTS

Dull facts are dead
facts.
Truth is fresh and
growing—
Any fact that bores
me
Isn't worth the
knowing.

FAILURE

It's not the things I
failed to do
That make me wipe
this eye—
It's things I should and
could have done
And simply failed
to try.

FAIR EXCHANGE

I'd never change places
with anyone else
No matter how sad I
might be,
And that's a good thing
because no one I'm sure
Would ever
change places
with me.

FAITH

Though groping through
illusions
I make my earnest
prayer
I'll never get beyond
them
And find there's
nothing
there.

FALLING LEAVES

The trees stand proud
against the sky.
They lose their leaves
with careless grace
I too should hold my
head up high
Whatever loss
I have
to face.

FALL POEM

Now the leaves are
falling,
Grey the autumn skies,
Southward geese are
calling,
Perish countless flies.

FALSE CONSOLATION

That it helps to think
of others
Who are much worse
off than me
Is a form of
consolation
I never quite
can see.

FALSE ECONOMY

We have to give
ourselves to life
Before we really live.
It's foolish hoarding
love or wealth —
They lose, who never
give.

FAME

Each tries to get his
  share of fame
In spite of modest
  disavowals —
Some carve their
  names in history,
And some embroider
  them on
  towels.

FAMILIAR THINGS

There are other things
  beside the things we see.
The most familiar room
  and bed and chair
At times if I surprise
  them suddenly
Are wearing
  like a cloak
  a secret air.

FANCY

In my fancy I appear
Well-groomed and
kindly and sincere,
Never holding spiteful
views
And never wearing
muddy shoes.

FATE

I sometimes think my
life will be
And has been since
my birth
A war my little ego
fights
With everything
on earth.

My mind is something
like a sieve—
Though lots of facts
run through it
I find when I
examine it
That very few
stick to it.

FAUCETS

The faucet leaks a
single drop
And like a tiny
wakeful bird
It chirps and tinkles
through the night
The smallest song I
ever heard.

FAULTS

The faults of my
  friends
Which I freely
  condone
Are always the ones
Which resemble
  my own.

FEAR

Do the thing you're
  most afraid of;
Never let it know you
  fear it.
Dangers only hurt
  the body
But it's fear
  that kills
  the spirit.

The price of shoes has
spoiled my life
Which once was calm
and sweet—
Although I slave the
livelong day
I cant support
my feet!

FELINE

A cat stared fixedly
at me
With solemn, knowing
eyes.
Our minds met in a
wordless pause—
And his mind seemed
more wise!

FENCES

When I consider Time
and Space
It fills me with a
quiet mirth
To see a human
fencing off
A tiny portion
of the
earth.

FIDGETY

My way of life's a
lazy one
Yet well enough it
serves —
I think that half
this busyness
Is just a form
of nerves.

How doth the busy
tourist
Go flitting 'round so
fast
Procuring blurry
snapshots
Of the wonders
of the past?

FINITE

The world is much too
large for me.
I wish that it were
small—
I hate to think I'll
have to leave
Before I see
it all.

FIRMNESS

Firm I stand through
storm and stress.
I know that it will
end.
I will not break
beneath my woe—
But goodness,
how I bend!

FISH

A fish seems very
sad to me —
No matter what its
trouble
It opens up its
mouth to moan
And just emits
a bubble.

FLATTERY

I thrive on admiration.
It stimulates my
mind—
We all might be
more brilliant
If everyone
were kind.

FLEA

My dog presented me
today
With just one little
flea.
He missed it not at all,
but, oh—
The difference
to me!

FLEETING PRESENT

I plan for the
  future,
I yearn for the
  past —
And meantime the
  present
Is leaving me fast.

FLIGHT

How marvelous are
  men these days.
They leave the earth
  and fly above it.
You can't keep down
  the human race —
I'm proud to be
  a member
  of it.

A little fly without
a care
Goes swimming through
the sun-drenched air.
It has a tiny song it
sings
And tiny rainbows on
its wings.

FLYING TIME

Time goes faster
every minute.
Days all telescope
together —
Years that once had
different seasons
Now are just
a streak
of weather.

FOAM

The tide of summer
rising,
A green wave strong
and dark,
Breaks in a foam of
blossoms
And children
in the park.

FOG

The fog comes
creeping quietly.
A sense of mystery
it brings,
And by half-hiding
it reveals
More beauty
in familiar
things.

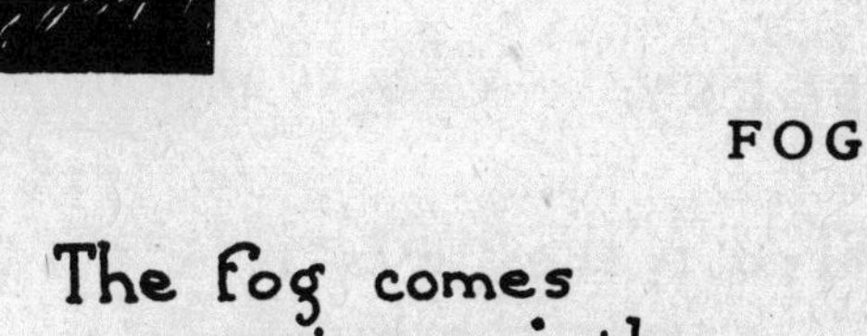

FOLKS

People sad or mad or
glad,
People wild or tame,
Looked at from a
mountain top
Seem about the
same.

FOLLY

Trust the joys life
gives to you.
Examine not the gift.
To analyze and test
each mood
Is mean, mistaken
thrift.

FOOD

When work seems
rather dull to me
And life is not so
sweet
One thing at least can
bring me joy —
I simply love
to eat!

FOOTPRINTS

I love a field of
smooth clean snow
Untouched by any
human feet.
And when I have to
walk through one
I try to make
my footprints
neat.

FORGETFULNESS

To seek my own small
  happiness
Is foolish, I begin
  to see—
It's when I quite
  forget myself
That happiness will
  come to me.

FORGIVENESS

I forgive all my
  enemies nobly
Because I'm so gentle
  and kind—
But to let them forget
  I forgive them
Is very much
  harder,
 I find.

FORMALITY

I'm friends with trees
and animals
As if I always knew
them —
Just humans seem to
think I need
An introduction
to them.

FOR SHOW

I like the simple joys
of life —
I haven't time to
taste them though
Because I have to
work so hard
To buy expensive
things
for show.

FRECKLES

The sun sent one of
his billion rays
Down ninety-three
million miles
To make this freckle
upon my nose —
A fact that
I think of
with smiles.

FREE LOVE

Love hurt my heart
until I saw
It never could be
owned by me,
But when I freely
gave my love
I found it set
my own heart
free.

FRENCH FLY

While riding to Paris
 from Havre on the train
I saw a small boy
 more excited than I—
When a fly began buzzing
 around on the pane:
"Oh, lookit," he cried,
"there's a little
 French fly!"

FRENCH PASTRY

Things are better
 than they seem
So the cheerful
 writers say—
Oftentimes french
 pastry though
Strikes me just the
 other way.

FRETTING

I ought to have more
faith in life,
Not fret because I'm
far from strong,
But do the day's
work as I can,
And life will
carry me
along.

FREUD

I was born a conservative
child.
All my deeds were quite
proper and mild.
But my lack of
transgression
They now call repression-
And so I must try
to be wild!

FRIENDLY POETS

I don't know any agony
That ever seems as
great to me
As hearing poets
whom I know
Get up and read
their poetry.

FRIENDS

We're here so short
a time before
We go to unknown
ends.
We may not meet
in other worlds,—
Let's hurry and
be friends.

FRIENDSHIP

Whenever I am
  plunged in woe
My true friends
  rally round,
So trouble is a
  friendship test
If nothing else,
  I've found.

FROGS

The friendly feeling
  that I have
For frogs is very
  strong—
I love their funny,
  pompous looks,
Their strange
  incessant
  song.

FROST

Last night the frost
was heavy,
And now the fields
are white
With shrouds of little
singers
Who chirped
their last,
last night.

FULL MEASURE

I'd gladly labor
underpaid
(Although I'm not, I
must admit)
But should I feel I'm
underpraised
You'd never hear
the last
of it.

FUNDAMENTALIST

"The world is all ahead
of you,"
My teachers used
to say—
And though I've grown
much older now
It seems
to stay
that way.

FUTILE REMORSE

Remorse is both futile
and weak
And also it's very
unpleasant—
Instead of regretting
my past
I'll concentrate
more on
my present.

FUTURE

With eyes on to-
morrow
I lope on my way.
I never touch earth,
for
I hurdle
today.

GAIETY

I love to feel a
summer day
Blow past me with
the breeze
While I'm as lazy
and as gay
As leafy,
laughing
trees.

GAIN

They say that youth's
the care-free time
But I have learned
with age this truth:
It's just by growing
old we gain
The wisdom to enjoy
our youth.

GAME

Well, life may not have
much meaning.
Blind chance seems to
rule each day—
But if you can take
it lightly
It's a pretty
good game
to play.

GAY BANNERS

My past is like a
banner gay,
A patterned web of
joy and sorrow,
I wave behind me as
I march
Through
thrilling days
to meet
tomorrow.

GENERATIONS

Oh, do you remember, a
few years ago
That young generation
that worried us so?
Well, now they are aging
and settled, poor things-
Be calm, worried critics,
for Time clips
all wings.

GENEROSITY

I can't afford
economy —
I save a dollar now
and then
Which makes me feel
so virtuous
I'm always moved to
squander ten.

GETTING ACROSS

Although when trouble
first appears
It seems so black
and wide
I plunge right in and
soon I find
I reach the other
side.

GIFT

I bargained with life
for her gladness.
I pared down the price
in my thrift,
Until I discovered this
secret—
Life's gladness is
always a
gift.

GIVING

It's not by hoarding
wealth or love
That man grows rich,
I see—
The more I freely
give to life
The more life gives
to me.

GLADNESS

When I'm sad all my sadness is centered in me.
The world just as happily passes me by.
But when I am glad all my gladness goes out
And feels just as big as the earth
and the sky.

GLOOM

How strange a place and remote from life
Is the dentist's reception room,
With its magazines that are ages old
And its feeling of timeless gloom!

GLOOMY AUTHORS

To gloomy, modern
authors
How drab the whole
world looks!
I'm glad life's more
romantic
Than "realistic"
books.

GOAL

I searched the world
for happiness
But sorrows met me
everywhere.
They drove me back
to my own heart—
And happiness was
waiting there.

GOATS

How I feel for those
goats in the mountains
Who leap over canyons
all day!
I go leaping from
pay day to pay day
The same insecure-
feeling way.

GOD'S ANGER

I'm always amused at
that grumbling sound
Of distant thunder
rolling around
And muttering threats
as if it hurled
A cosmic grouch
against the
world.

GOLDEN SILENCE

Though lacking in
small talk
I feel no dismay—
I'll simply look deep
when
I've nothing to say.

GOLF

I'm taking up the game
of golf—
I use my mashie with
such force
I heard a catty person
say
I'm also
taking up
the course.

GOODNESS

I know I'm often
cross and small
With thoughts like
sand burs in my mind.
Why will I treat
myself like that?
I'm happy
only when
I'm kind.

GOOSE-STEP

When I object to
styles I see
"That's what they're
wearing," salesmen say,
And then I buy for
well I know
That I must
dress the
same as
"they."

GOSSIP

I heard some talk
about myself,
And most unfair it
seemed to be —
Oh, well, I live in my
own mind
And not in others'
thoughts
of me.

GRACEFUL WEAKNESS

I lack decision in my
life —
Well, if I can't be
firm and strong,
Like wind-blown flowers
I'll bow with grace
To any fate
that comes
along.

GRAIN OF SALT

Although I keep a diary
I don't record my
smallest fault,
So when I read about
my past
I take it with a
grain of salt.

GRASSY HILL

I wish I had a little
grassy hill
With weeds and bees and
one grey sun-warmed stone
Where I could go and sit
and think all day —
I want one
piece of earth
my very own.

GREATNESS

City of the soaring
heights,
Of crystal, steel and
flashing lights,
Can it possibly be true
That little men
like us
made you?

GREED

Work should never
make me weary
If I'm really meant
to do it,
But it soon becomes
exhausting
If it's greed that
drives me
to it.

GREETINGS

From our chilly, little
home
With lips and noses
blue
We send the warmest
thing we have—
Our Christmas
wish to you.

GREY HAIR

I never feel much
older
Though grey I grow
and sere,
But somehow other
people
Seem younger
every year.

GRIEF

Though present sorrow
feels as if
Forever it will last
How foolish, brief and
small our woes
Appear when they
are past!

GRIT

Have faith in yourself
when the world
Seems determined to
break your endurance—
You often can bluff a
hard fate
If you meet it with
nerve and
assurance.

GROWTH

Growth means constant
change
So only those who dare
To do things new and
strange
Are getting
anywhere.

GUEST

Speak gently to the
dinner guest,
Nor chide him when
he's late,
For some time you
yourself may be
In his
unhappy
state.

GUIDING LIGHTS

I love to be out in the
woods at night
But the wind makes
a spooky sound—
I wish I could tame
a few lightning bugs
And get them
to lead me
around.

HALOES

The sun shines through
the curtains,
Diffused, serenely
bright,
And common things
wear halos,
Caressed
with lovely
light.

HAND AND BRAIN

The rhythm of life
seems more sure,
More freely my spirit
expands,
If after I've worked
with my mind
I work for awhile
with my
hands.

HANGOVER

After the banquet
last night
Such a nightmare I had
it still lingers —
And I sit in the wrong
kind of clothes
And clutch the wrong
fork in my
fingers!

HAPPINESS

The richest of men
I haven't a doubt
Counts his wealth
by the things
He is happy without.

HAPPY MEDIUM

I mustn't live too
greedily —
I'll make each
small joy last,
And not weigh down
my future with
An undigested
past.

HAPPY NEW YEAR

The new year follows
on the old
Without a moment's
breathing space.
Twelve solemn strokes
the clock just tolled—
Well, happy
New Year,
human race!

HAPPY POET

I can't write a verse—
I'm too happy today
With a sudden,
ridiculous glee.
If the spring's in your
heart as it is in mine
You don't need
a poem
from me!

HAPPY THOUGHT

When I think a happy
thought
It colors everything
I see.
It sends out rays to
touch the world
And everything
shines back
at me.

HARDENED

The heart that is
hardened to sorrow,
Refusing to share the
world's grief,
Will be hardened to
gladness tomorrow—
Or such is my righteous
belief.

This thought when I
am laboring
Has made my efforts
greater —
The hardest things
I do right now
Will make life easy
later.

HARD JOB

Be good, the wholesome
poet said,
And let who will be
clever —
I'm here to say the
second job's
The harder one
however.

HATS

I love the hats I
see in shops
But when they're home
I cannot bear them.
They're still all right
but I'm all wrong—
I wish I didn't
have to
wear them.

HATS OFF

The sun shines in the
springtime
With light so warm
and kind
That when I take my
hat off
I feel it on
my mind.

HAVEN

I'll build a tower in
  my mind
Of all the beauty that
  I know—
When life seems ugly
  then I'll have
A high and secret
  place to go.

HEADS

When we consider
  Providence
We must admit it's
  fair,
For some are given
  brilliant minds
While some
  have curly
  hair.

HEALTH

Whene'er I have a
tragic woe
I feel I should be
thin and white.
I never look the part
I know—
I cannot lose my
appetite.

HEARTS

We can't be detached
from the race.
United we stand or
we fall.
And every sad heart
in the world
Is felt just a little
by all.

HEIGHTS

Sometimes I feel larger
than all the world.
I look at it calmly
from god-like heights-
And space is a tent with
the sky pinned down,
And time is a flicker
of days
and nights.

HELPFUL MISFORTUNES

I learn from all my
failures.
In later days I see
It's often my
misfortunes
That did the
most for me.

HELPING HAND

Instead of envying
our friends
Their greater riches
and success
We'd make our own
seem greater too
By helping those
we know
with less.

HELPING OTHERS

To know that others
suffer too
Is not much comfort
in my woe,
But if I try to help
them, then
My own small troubles
swiftly go.

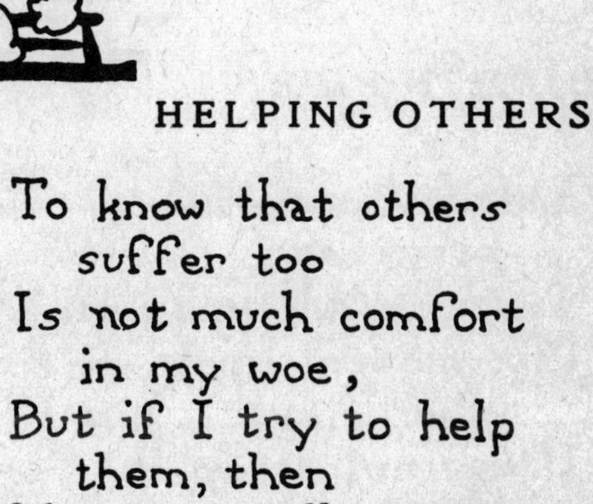

HERO

Although a safe
contented life
Brings peace and
happiness to some
A wilder deeper joy
is found
In dangers
bravely
overcome.

HIDDEN LIFE

I love to tell my
secrets.
I do it all unbidden.
My hidden life's so
thrilling
I cannot keep it
hidden.

HIDDEN POWERS

All men are richer than
they think—
With patient search
you'll find
New powers you've never
used before
Still sleeping in your
mind.

HIGHBROW

I read the deepest
books there are.
They never help me
much I know.
My mind can't hold so
many facts—
I like to say I've
read them
though.

I sort of flounder
through my days,
Losing money, missing
cars—
I keep my mind on
higher things
And thus I
get some
awful jars.

HILLS

Human joys change.
Unchanging are
these:
The friendship of
hills,
The soft
songs of
trees.

HILLTOP

With all this lovely
time and space
Around me everywhere
Why should I clutter
up my life
With hurry,
toil and
care.

HOARDING

If you hoard your
wealth of course
You'll have it for a
rainy day,
But if you hoard your
love you'll find
That it has
vanished
all away.

HOLES

Oh, the raisins they put
in rice pudding are few,
And few are the oysters
they put in the stew—
But you'll have to admit
that in contrast to these
They always put plenty
of holes in
the cheese.

HOLIDAYS

Poets now all welcome
spring
While winter leaves
with scanty praise,
Yet give a thought to
winter too—
At least it's
full of
holidays.

HOME

I love to roam in
  summer,
By distant hills
  invited,
But home is best in
  winter,
Warm and
  golden-
  lighted.

HONESTY

Oh, why did I in loud
  firm tones
Just when the room
  grew still
Say, "Don't you hate
  dull teas like this?
They almost
  make me
  ill!"

HOPE

My hope springs up
in spite of blows,
Higher after every
fall.
Down the road of
life it goes
Bounding like
a rubber
ball.

HORIZONS

"When I get rich" the
children dream
With eyes on some
far day.
And when they're old,
with eyes turned back:
"When I was rich"
they say.

HOSTS

All summer were welcomed
by seashore and woods.
They give us their
sunniest smile—
But they seem just a
little relieved in the fall
That they'll be
by themselves
for awhile.

HOURGLASS

I ought to make the
most of time
And gather days in
fruitful sheaves—
The unused minutes of
my life
Just drop away like
withered leaves.

HOUSE CLEANING

At intervals I clean my
 bureau drawers
And treasures long mis-
 laid I always find—
I might discover precious
 thoughts like that
By clearing old
 confusions
 from my
 mind.

HOUSES

We all live in houses
 of thought
Life builds in our
 minds so it seems—
The walls and the
 floors are just facts,
But the windows and
 doors are
our dreams.

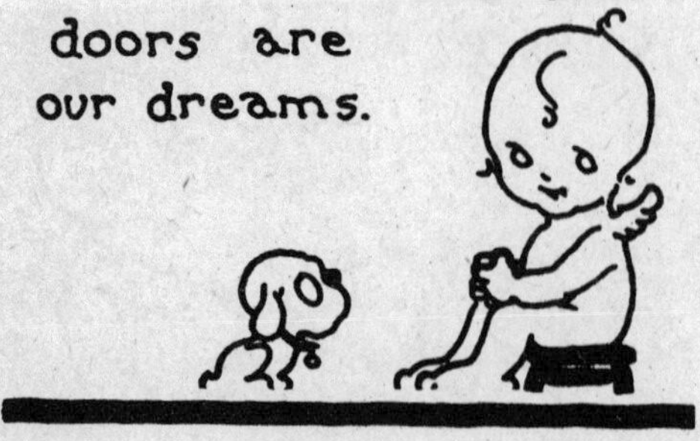

HUMANE THOUGHT

Be kind to all dumb
  animals
And give small birds
  a crumb.
Be kind to human
  beings too—
They're sometimes
  pretty dumb.

HUMANITY

The human race
  delights me so.
It's silly, but I
  love it—
I hardly ever stop
  to think
That I'm a member
  of it.

HUMAN RACE

One thing at least I've
 learned from life —
You cannot change the
 human race :
You think you've got it
 all repressed
When up it bobs some
 other place.

HUMAN TOUCH

It's nice the human
 race can laugh —
I've always noticed in
 a crowd
That total strangers
 feel like friends
If something
 makes them
laugh aloud.

HUMBLENESS

More than I long for
wealth
(And I've never been
one to flout it)
Do I long for the kind
of soul
That contentedly
does
without it.

HUMOR

Humor is based upon
courage.
Man with his undaunted
will,
Surrounded by countless
misfortunes,
Can laugh at
his destiny
still.

HURDY-GURDY

I have a hurdy-gurdy
mind
That grinds out verse
on this and that.
Come rain or shine I
never stop—
I'd like a
penny in
my hat.

HURRAH

I did the thing I
feared the most.
Excuse me while I
cheer.
Now here I stand, a
stronger soul—
And all I've
lost is
fear.

HURRY

To live with leisure
every day
Makes time seem endless,
calm and vast.
It's only when I rush
myself
That time as well
goes rushing
past.

HURT VANITY

I quite forgive my
enemies
To show my great
humanity
But find it harder to
forgive
The friends
who hurt
my vanity.

I fall so short of my
ideal
At times I'm almost
moved to cry:
"Don't judge me, please,
by what I do—
This small cross
person
isn't I!"

IGNORANCE

It's funny how little
I know.
My mind is quite
empty of facts.
I really don't think
much at all—
I live more
in feelings
and acts.

IMAGINARY PORTRAIT

The proofs that
  photographers send
Are much more
  revealing than kind.
That's not how I look
  to myself—
I'm always
  retouched,
in my mind!

IMAGINATION

Although I must trudge
  through the world on
    my feet
My mind can cast off
  human bars,
And often at night it
  goes zipping around
And skimming
  up handfuls
  of stars.

IMMUNITY

I covet not riches
Or fame high and
bright,
But I envy those
people
Mosquitoes don't bite.

IMPORTANCE

I'm always losing
rubbers
And breaking package
strings —
Oh, the horrible
importance
Of unimportant
things.

IMPROVIDENCE

Ants are such dull
little insects,
Grubbing and saving
all day,
Butterflies never
can teach them
Life is for beauty
and play.

IMPULSE

I'd like to hug the
human race
So much I feel that I
adore it
But if I tried this on
the street
I s'pose I'd
get arrested
for it.

INCLINATION

Some people slave for
 money
With all their youth
 and health
While some are rich
 in leisure —
There are many kinds
 of wealth.

INCONSISTENCY

I'm sure I have a
 noble mind
And honesty and tact,
And no one's more
 surprised than I
To see the way
 I act!

INDEPENDENCE DAY

Since this is
Independence Day
And also very hot
Why should I write
a verse at all—
I'd really
rather not.

INDIFFERENCE

Though life is sometimes
sad and hard
Because it's life I
love it.
I've noticed woe will
often go
If I just say,
"What of it?"

INDIFFERENTLY BAD

First I'm bad and then
I'm good.
I thus relieve the
tedium—
And if I add my two
extremes
I strike a happy
medium.

INERTIA

With songs the
energetic birds
All greet the break
of day—
I certainly would give
a lot
If I could feel
that way.

INFERIORITY

I'd like to be so
beautiful
That people always
stared at me
But, as it is, if
people do
I think it's
something
wrong they
see!

INGRATITUDE

We throw our papers on
the grass.
We tear up flowers, and
act like pests —
Of all the creatures
on the earth
We're Nature's
most ungrateful
guests.

INNER LIFE

Nothing that happens
can hurt me
Whether I lose or
I win —
Though life may be
changed on the surface
I do my main living
within.

INNOCENCE

The history of all the
world
With war and greed is
weighted,
But somehow though I
live here too
I don't feel
implicated.

INSECTS

The meadow seems all
peace to me—
Yet cross black ants
are fighting there,
And fat bewildered
beetles run
On desperate errands,
filled with
care.

INSOMNIA

I cannot go to
sleep.
I'm never rested
fully—
I count so many
sheep
My mind is getting
wooly.

INSULT

Last summer we roasted
and soon we shall freeze
While blizzards scream
round us exulting—
The weather the poor
human race must endure
Seems to me
nothing short
of insulting.

INTENTIONS

The noblest of impulses
spring from my heart.
That I'm helpful and kind
there is never a doubt.
My plans are all made
for the good of the race,
But I find it's a
bother to
carry them out.

INTERRUPTIONS

Interruptions steal
my time,
And callers make me
run and hide—
When I am in the
mood to work
I want the world to
stand aside.

INTRODUCTION

Sometimes I see a
stranger's face
That looks so sad or
filled with fright
I want to speak and
try to help—
Alas, I can't;
it's not
polite.

I ought to trace my
motives
To the bottom of
my mind —
It's good for me, but
often
It's embarrassing,
I find.

INVENTORY

One day I took stock
of my faults —
Such dozens and dozens
I had
I could never be good,
But I easily could
Be perfectly,
dazzlingly
bad.

IRRITATIONS

All of life's great
crises
I have the strength
to meet —
It's little irritations
That bring me sure
defeat.

I TOLD YOU SO

The strangest people
that I know
Are those who say,
"I told you so"
As if they felt a
grim delight
To find their dark
forebodings
right.

JAM

When your day gets in
a jam
With twice the work for
which you've time
Desert it for a
matinee —
It's on the
way to one
that I'm!

JANUARIES

Each year I swear I'll
keep a diary.
It's sad my resolutions
never last —
To read them you might
think I'd only had
A bunch of Januaries
in my past!

If your job is work
to you
Quit it, I am here
to say —
Find the work you're
meant to do
And it won't
be work
but play.

JOKE

I was called upon once
for a speech.
I thought I was doing
it well
Till I couldn't
remember the point
Of a joke
that I started
to tell.

JOURNAL

I like to keep a
journal
Of work and play
and weather —
It makes each day
important
And holds my life
together.

JOY

Life itself can't give
me joy
Unless I really will
it.
Life just gives me
time and space —
It's up to me
to fill it.

JOYFUL

If I can love all life
My troubles soon
depart —
The world reflects
the joy
I carry in my
heart.

JOY REMEMBERED

Perhaps there is no
perfect joy.
It comes but soon it's
gone —
Still hope and memory
at least
Go living on
and on.

JOYS

I love the little joys
of life —
The smell of rain,
the sound of brooks,
The taste of crispy
toast and jam,
The sight of rows
and rows
of books.

JUDGMENT

I'll try to see my
friends' mistakes
With kind and under-
standing eye,
And never judge the
things they do
Until I know the
reasons why.

JUST DESERTS

Time sorts people out
Whatever they
pretend,
And just the fame
they've earned
It gives them in
the end.

JUSTICE

I'd rather be mean
to a person
Than mean to a dog
or a cat,
For people can tell
a policeman
And animals cannot
do that.

KINDNESS

Let us help our
fellow man
When conveniently
we can—
How smoothly all the
world would run
If we were kind to
everyone!

KINGS

Why should I envy
the great?
Each man has a
place of his own.
I myself am a
whole little world
Where I'm ruler,
and sit on
a throne.

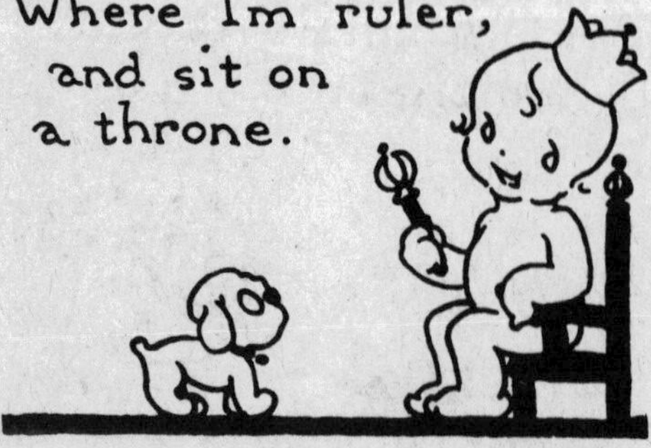

KINSHIP

It helps me when my
past misdeeds
Flock round and haunt
me with disgrace
To think this secret
sense of guilt
Is felt by all the
human race.

KISS

I made the nicest
kiss I could
And blew it to the
moon so far,
And then I watched
the empty sky
And pop —
out came a
little star!

KITCHEN

I've cleaned the kitchen
white as snow
And I intend to keep
it neat —
We'll have to eat in
restaurants,
Or else we
simply
cannot eat

KNIGHTS

No more do gallant
knights ride out
On chargers bold
with banners gay —
But many just as
noble knights
Charge forth
on street cars
every day.

KNOW THYSELF

We only find ourselves
In everything we
see—
The more new friends
I know
The more I'll learn
of me.

LACK

The human race varies
in marvelous ways.
We are clever and
foolish and deep.
In only one thing we're
alike it would seem—
We never have had
enough sleep.

LADIES

How smooth and pleasant
ladies are!
Their surfaces, are
never changed
Unless they hear a
shocking truth
And get their
features
disarranged.

LAKES

The lake holds lives
unknown to me,
Cold, loveless lives the
sun can't reach—
A dim strange world
I'll never see
Laps at my
feet upon
the beach!

LARGER LIFE

An impulse toward a
larger life
Should be obeyed at
any cost.
Of course it's safer
not to dare,
But think of
all the life
youve lost.

LASTING HAPPINESS

You cannot make your
happiness
Depend on things that
others do.
You'll always find the
lasting kind
Depends on no one
else but
you.

LAST LAUGH

Pride shall not govern
my acts.
Than public opinion
I'm stronger.
He who laughs last
may laugh best
But he who
laughs first
can laugh
longer.

LAST STRAWS

Sometimes life seems
so crushing
That I think my
strength will break.
Now some one's used
my inkwell
For an ash tray
by mistake.

LAST YEAR

I write these verses
'way ahead.
It makes it seem so
queer —
Though now it's nineteen
twenty-five
I wrote these words
last year.

LATE

I'm always late to
everything.
My friends are most
sarcastic.
I wish that it could
be arranged
That time
were more
elastic.

LAUGH

I'm often more clever
and catty than kind
It's such a temptation
to show off my mind,
But if to gain laughter
I hurt a good friend
It's plain that the laugh
is on me
in the end.

LAUGHTER

Nothing can stand
against laughter—
Mark Twain made this
wise remark first—
And time and again I
have proved it
When things were
about at
their worst.

LAWN MOWER

The mower whirs
across the lawn.
It makes for me a
homesick sound—
I long to be a child
again
And throw the fragrant
grass around.

LAWS

Nature makes one set
of rules
For which she seems
to have just cause.
Then man, supremely
impudent,
Tries thwarting her
with little
laws.

LAWS WANTED

We either freeze or
else we roast —
Reformers ought to
get together
And if they want to
do some good
Just pass a
law against
the weather.

LAZINESS

I'm ready for
adventure
Where death and
danger lurk,
For sacrifice or
daring,
Or anything
but work.

LAZY

I can't believe it's
morning
That has come so cold
and soon—
The world must
manage somehow
If I stay in bed
till noon.

LAZY BONES

I'd face my life with
strong brave heart
If I could have one
priceless boon—
That I might skip
these frosty dawns
And have my day
begin at
noon.

LEADEN FEET

As I grow old time flies
so fast
I almost hear it
humming—
It's very strange that
pay day though
Is just as slow
in coming.

LEADERS

Each man who bravely
fights his way,
Who tackles problems
with a vim,
Adds just a little to
the strength
Of all those
coming
after him.

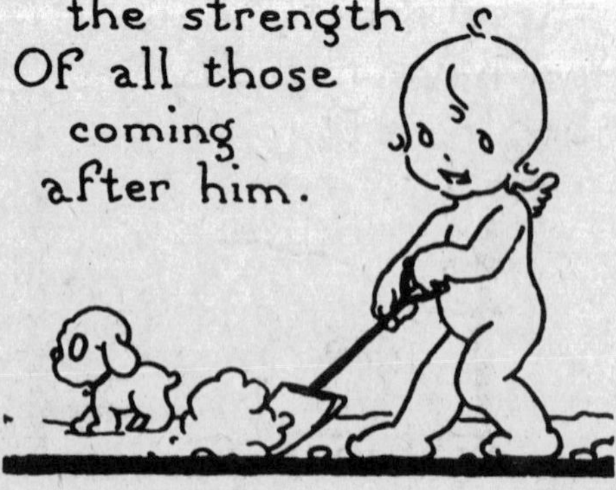

LEAVES

I love to shuffle
through the woods
When leaves are brown
and ankle-deep.
They sing a crinkly
drowsy song
Before they
settle down
to sleep.

LEGENDS

Tales of the brave deeds
of old
Fill us with wonder
today —
What legends of us
will be told
Hundreds of years
away?

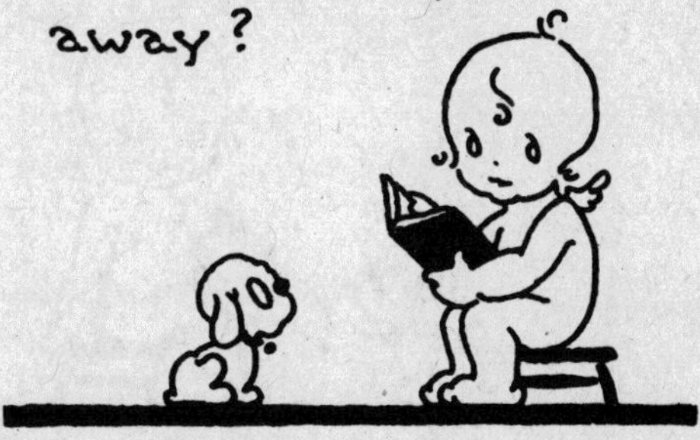

To live with leisure
every day
And never fret or
worry
Will make each hour
twice as long—
No one has
time to
hurry.

LENIENCY

Well, since the world's
a large wild place
And often inconvenient,
We might among
ourselves at least
Be friendly, kind
and lenient.

LIES

The man who tells or
acts small lies
In word or deed had
best beware—
He'll lose himself
among his fibs
Till pretty soon he
isn't there!

LIFE

Life is very simple.
We dress in cloth
and leather,
And laugh and cry
a little
Among a lot of
weather.

Stained glass windows
 make the light
Like songs of beauty
 from the sun.
Life could shine
 through us like that,
You and
 me and
 everyone.

LIGHT AND SHADE

If half the world is
 shadow
Half at least is
 light,
And joy comes after
 sorrow
As day comes
 after night.

LIGHT OCCUPATION

The joys fate means
for me will come
And yet I'm here to
state
The hardest thing I
ever did
Was just to sit
and wait.

LIGHT WORDS

Words fall as lightly
as snow.
They're easily,
thoughtlessly said—
Yet hard words can
enter the heart
And lie there
as heavy
as lead.

LIKENESS

I went to get my
photograph
But just as things
began:
"Do you want a pretty
picture, or
A likeness?" said
the man!

LINKS

The daily chain of
circumstance
And all my thoughts
so interlink
And each affects the
other so—
I think it's lots of
fun to
think!

LITTLE THINGS

Small irritations
Like dust in the
eye
Can blind us to big
things
As life hurries by.

LITTLE TRIUMPHS

Although my troubles
seem as black
And big at times as
night
The little triumphs
that I have
Can make the
whole world
bright.

I cannot hurry fate
Or hold it back a
minute,
But I can live each
day
For everything
that's in it.

LOAFING

The joy of a day's
work done
Is a joy that I
have tasted —
But better than that
I like
The joy of a day
well wasted.

LOCUSTS

The locusts have a
rasping call.
They saw the air
with sound —
The drowsy summer
minutes fall
In tatters to the
ground.

LOGIC

In all the things I
do in life
The way that others
view them
Should matter not as
much to me
As reasons why I
do them.

LONELINESS

Am I the only one in
life
Who always seems to
stand apart
Or is it everyone
who feels
A little lonesome
in his heart?

LONGING

It's foolish to be
longing
For adventures far
away —
For if I'm ready
for them
I'll find new
thrills
each day.

LONG PANTS

The wisdom of the
youthful
It's hard indeed to
measure —
In being bitter
cynics
They take
a childish
pleasure.

LONG THOUGHTS

I like to think long
thoughts at night
When all the talk
and bustle ends.
I lie and gossip with
myself
About my strange
amusing friends.

LOOKING BACKWARD

When I am feeling
  sad I find
I'm looking backward
  in my mind,
For sorrows never
  really last
Unless we won't
  let go
the past.

LOOKING FORWARD

My future seems
  uncertain.
With problems I'm
  perplexed—
Oh, well, I'll still
  look forward
To the future after
  next.

LOSING CAUSE

The one who sticks to
a losing cause
Although his fortunes
get a fall
May find that, gaining
strength and pride,
He's not the
loser after
all.

LOSS

Bare trees against
the winter sky
Make patterns delicate
as lace.
Thus loss can give
the strong of soul
A special kind
of charm
and grace.

LOST DAY

Snow comes falling
through the day.
Behind the snow the
sky is grey.
Behind the sky, shut
off from me,
Is one day's
sun I'll
never see.

LOST LABORS

When you work for the
thing you believe in
You're rich though the
whole way is rough—
But work that is simply
for money
Will never quite pay
you enough.

LOST OPPORTUNITIES

As o'er my past my
eyes I cast
It's not my crimes
that I regret—
The times I failed to
take a chance
Are those I wish I
might forget.

LOVE

A man can own uncounted
gold
And land and buildings
tall,
But love is just to
give away—
It can't be
owned
at all.

LOVE AFFAIR

The spring comes bearing
gifts for all,
She brings new leaves
for trees to wear,
New songs for birds,
new hats for girls—
For me a
brand new
love affair.

LOVING-KINDNESS

Though fate may seem
to be unkind
There's nothing that is
past forgiving
Because all life is
built upon
An undefeated
love of
living.

LOWLINESS

I can be gay all day
long
Filling my unremarked
place,
Singing my little flat
song
That dies right in
front of
my face.

LUCIDITY

It helps when troubles
seem so large
They simply fill our
hearts with fear
To take them as a
mental test
And get our thoughts
about them
clear.

LUCK

I saw a four-leaf
clover
The which I stooped
to pluck,
And then a rude bee
stung me —
I don't call
that good
luck.

LUXURY

I'm glad my life is
hard at times
Although I can't
luxuriate —
If everything were
soft for me
I might sink
in and
suffocate.

MACHINE AGE

Inventions add more
speed to life:
Our words fly faster
through the air,
And ships and trains
and aeroplanes
All hurl us faster on—
but where?

MAGIC

Life's little
irritations
At times seem
blackly tragic
But see them in
proportion
And they disappear
like magic.

Big tragedies I nobly
face.
I think how fine and
brave it looks.
And yet I'm floored
by little things
Like missing cars
and losing
cooks.

MAILMAN

When I think of our
fine postal service
With wonder and pride
my mind fills —
They seldom if ever
lose letters
And never,
oh, never
lose bills!

MAN

Although I pity ancient
man,
(We're luckier than
he),
I hate to think
posterity
Will some day
pity me!

MANANA

Ambition burns within
my heart.
I feel my powers
all expand—
There's nothing that
I wouldn't do
Except the job
that's right
at hand.

Plants and beasts
so unreflecting
Live on earth without
a care.
Why should worried
human beings
Run distracted
here and
there?

MANNERS

At parties although I am
bitterly bored
I act just as pleased as
I can all the while—
And so when the world
hands me sorrowful
times
I ought to
remember my
manners,
and smile.

MARTYR

The old-time family
martyr
I intend to have
suppressed—
I want no sacrifices
Forced upon me by
this pest.

MASKS

Along the street the
people walk.
They look complacent,
free and wise—
And yet I sometimes
think I see
A prisoner
behind their
eyes.

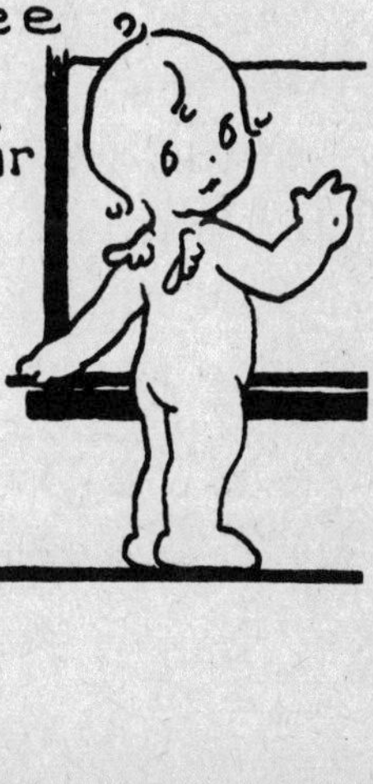

MASTERING FATE

The lover of life is
always safe.
He knows no complete
disaster.
For since he gladly
accepts his fate
Of fate itself he is
master.

MATURITY

I used to roller-skate
in spring.
Tall trees I used
to climb.
I wasn't through with
such pursuits —
I've just been
tricked
by Time!

MAZE

Details blind me to
my life.
I'm simply living in
a maze—
I'm busied so with
this and that
I hardly see
myself
for days.

ME

I feel so thrillingly
alive
And filled with vim
and glee
It's strange to think
that years ago
There wasn't
any me!

MEALS

The meals that stretch
all down my life
Appall me when I
look ahead —
The lakes of soup and
hills of meat
I'll have to eat before
I'm dead!

MEDES

I hear of the Medes
and Persians
But never pay much
heed —
I don't believe I
could mention
A single, prominent
Mede!

MEDIOCRITY

I'm doomed to
mediocrity.
It's this that makes
me sad —
I find I can't be
very good
Or even
very bad.

MEEKNESS

I'm sure I have a
brave stern soul
That naught in life
can override —
But when I meet folks
on the walk
It's always me
who turns
aside

MEMORY

My memory's like a
spider's web
That holds bright joys
like drops of dew,
With here and there
an awful rent
Where whole
long weeks
have fallen
through.

MENDING

When clouds are dark
just get to work.
You'll never help by
whining—
A stitch in time, I
always say,
Will mend a
silver lining.

MENTAL VICTORIES

My life seems
uneventful
But only to the
blind
Who cannot see the
triumphs
I'm having in
my mind.

METAPHYSICS

I sit and think 'midst
toil and strife
My abstract, sweeping
thoughts on life.
My mind is much too
vague and grand
To cope with problems
near at
hand.

MICROSCOPE

Sitting far above the
town
High in a window,
looking down,
I sometimes see with
quite a jar
How much like
little bugs
we are!

MIDDLE YEARS

I'll never try with
creams and dye
To check grey hair
and wrinkled skin,
But rather guard my
heart against
An aging
caution
creeping in.

MILLIONAIRES

I never envy
millionaires
Their wealth and
motor cars —
I'd like to be a poet
though
For they
own all
the stars.

MIND

A little loose bundle
of memories,
A few of the simplest
of facts —
This is the thing that
I call my mind
That steers me
through all
of my acts!

One minor joy I have
in fall
Almost too small to
speak about—
It's after rain to
step on leaves
And see the
water
spurting out.

MIRROR

I passed a mirror in
the hall.
My face looked far
away and small—
And swept away on
Time's swift sea
I waved a quick
goodby
to me.

MISCAST

If all the world is
  just a stage
I'd like to wear a
  royal gown
And have the spotlight
  follow me —
But Fate has cast me
  for a
  clown.

MISER

On just one precious
  thing
Not all my love
  must fall,
For if I spread it
  out
I cannot lose it
  all.

MISFORTUNE

Misfortune flies around
 the world.
Unreasoning its darts
 it flings.
Perhaps it hits me—
 I don't know—
I fill my mind
 with other
 things.

MISSED?

I work in such a frenzy
That I almost have
 a fit,
And yet I sometimes
 wonder
Who would notice if
 I quit.

MISTAKES

I'd rather make
mistakes at times,
(For even in mistakes
I live)
Than be afraid to
take a risk
And make my whole
life negative.

MODE

Cold is the weather
and sleety
Yet gaily I whistle
and sing
To see in the
milliners' windows
The very first
signs of
the spring.

MODERATION

We shouldn't live at
  such high speed.
I simply will not
  do it —
I like my life a lot
  too well
To want to hurry
  through it.

MODESTY

I only want payment
For doing my task —
And wealth, fame
  and beauty
Are all that I ask.

MONEY

To work all day long
just for money
Mid turmoil and
hurry and strife
Might make me a
pretty good living
But wouldn't make
much of
a life.

MONKEYS

I stood before the
monkeys' cage,
Their funny ways
to see —
I laughed at them
a lot until
I saw one
laugh
at me.

MONOTONY

I claim imagination,
But that's an idle
boast
When every day
for breakfast
I eat an egg and
toast.

MOODS

A specialist in moods
am I.
I love each new
sensation—
And nothing makes me
feel so good
As righteous
indignation.

MOON

The moon who used to
thrill me so
Has lost her youthful
spell—
I never thought when
I grew old
That she'd
grow old
as well.

MOONLIGHT

The moon gets all
its brightness
From the sun's reflected
rays.
That's why its light
is eerie—
It's made
of ghosts
of days.

MORALS

I envy movie heroes
bold
And large-eyed heroines
as well.
They know so clearly
right from wrong—
A thing I often
cannot tell.

MOSQUITOES

God made the star-
hung skies for us,
And singing trees and
hills and lakes.
Of course He made
mosquitoes too—
But everybody
makes
mistakes.

MOTH

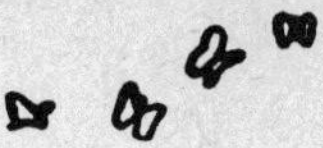

A moth is such a
fairy thing,
So lightly through
the air it floats—
Who'd think that it
subsisted on
Our heavy winter
overcoats!

MOTORING

I have a little flivver
That goes up and down
with me,
And how we stay
together so
Is more than I
can see.

MOTTO

I've made a rule to
win success.
I'll try to keep it in
my heart.
It's something anyone
can do:
Just finish
everything
you start.

MOTIVES

I can fail in my aims
and not mind
When I've labored the
best that I could—
But I cannot be calm
and resigned
When my motives
are not
understood.

MUDDLE

When problems come
and worry me
I nearly always
find
The muddle isn't in
the facts
So much as in
my mind.

MURDER

Some people speak
of killing time.
I don't know any
greater crime.
With work and beauty
they might fill it—
And yet they sit
around and
kill it.

I'd like to go where
music grows —
While violin notes
blew my hair
I'd wander through
the organ groves
And gather little
grace notes
there.

MUSIC'S CHARM

At concerts looking
round the hall
I see the dull, the
sad of face
And think the music
holds us all
Regardless, in a
perfect place.

MY ACTS

I will not let my
grievous past
With vain remorse
torment me —
I can't help feeling
that my acts
Don't really
represent me.

MY BEST

To give my very best
to life
Should be my greatest
aim —
It helps me too, for
when I do
Life gives
me back
the same.

MY JOB

A job too big I
cannot do.
A job too small
would bore me—
But surely somewhere
in the world
My job is
waiting
for me.

MYSELF

When I look in the
glass
A stranger I see
Who surely can't
know
How it feels
to be me!

MY SOUL

Who'd think to see
my plodding feet
And plain though
useful face
I have a gay and
dancing soul
That flits
from place
to place?

MYSTERY

Often across long
miles of space
Strange voices speak
strange words to me.
It brings such mystery
to life
When central makes
mistakes,
you see.

MY TIME

My possessions belong
to my friends
But I must have it
known,
Though freely I'd part
with my wealth,
That my time
is my own.

MY WORST ENEMY

No enemy or lurking
woe
Or sudden sore
distress
Has ever hurt my
life as much
As my own
laziness.

NAGGING WOES

Detached from all my
nagging woes
Upon a lofty peak I
stand—
If they'd detach
themselves from me
The situation
would be
grand.

NARROW-MINDED

Truth grows as we do,
year by year.
We change it with
our words and acts—
But narrow-minded
people stall,
Obstructing life with
last year's
facts.

NAVIGATION

The sailor has no
  harder job
Who sails the stormy
  oceans
Than I who steer
  my little soul
Through
strange and
deep emotions.

NEGLECT

Whenever I have
  cause to feel
That life's neglecting
  me a bit
I find the only
  reason is
That I'm not giving
  much to it.

NEGLIGENCE

We must respect the work we do.
A slipshod method never pays—
It may get by, but in our minds
It makes a scar that always stays.

NEIGHBOR

Though usually I spend my time
By my own life engrossed
It's when I'm helping others live
I feel I'm living most.

90.

I will not cling to
joys when Fate
Demands that I forsake
them —
Life always brings
new gifts to those
Whose hands
are free to
take them.

NEW GLADNESS

Some new gladness
always comes
To cheer me when my
spirit's low —
And likewise often
when it's high
Along will come
another blow.

NERVES

I swear that I'll
relax today.
My nerves are
simply overtaxed—
Right now I'm all
worked up and tense
I'm trying so to be
relaxed.

NEW DAY

I hate all habits,
good or bad.
They make life seem
so stale —
I'll live each day a
fresh new way
No matter how
I fail.

NEW JOY

The joy of life is hard
  to kill.
Its roots go deep in
  people's hearts.
Cold winds may freeze
  its bloom — but soon
From sturdy roots a new
  joy starts.

NEW LOVE

Some new love should
  take the place
Of every love
  departed —
For sorrow cannot
  fill your heart
Unless you're
  hollow-hearted.

NIGHT-TIME

The warm days lightly
skim the earth
Like smiles upon a
face,
But night goes deeper,
to its heart,
A dark and
silent place.

NIRVANA

Nearly all the war
and woe
With which my days
I fill
I might so easily
escape
By simply keeping
still.

NO REGRETS

I won't regret my
  past mistakes
Although they cost me
  dearly —
I cannot blame myself
  unless
I've acted
  insincerely.

NOT GUILTY

I overlook my past
  mistakes,
Excuse them and
  condone them —
Or, if they hurt my
  self-esteem,
With firmness I
  disown them.

NOTHING LASTS

Misfortune is never a
permanent thing.
It passes as soon as
it's here —
And we give it most
of the power it has
By worry about it
and fear.

NOW

The past before I
came seems dull,
The distant future
grey and drear —
The only warm and
colored time
Is just the
time that
I'll be here.

OBJECTION

These books on "How to
Win Success"
Have left my problems
all unsolved—
They sound inspiring,
but I find
There's always too
much work
involved.

OCEAN

It's strange when in
a storm at sea
At which my courage
fails
To think this ocean
even now
Is home, sweet home,
to whales.

OH, WELL

I can accept the fate
of each tomorrow.
A rootless gladness
blooms above my sorrow.
Across my life, a field
that bears no seed,
Go bobbing
little joys like
tumble-weed.

OLD AGE

There is no such thing
as old age I believe.
In the long race with time I
am sure we're all winning.
The closer we draw to
the end of things here
The nearer we are to
some other
beginning.

ONE FRIEND

Don't try to flee your
loneliness.
You'll only find it in
the end.
Just get acquainted
with yourself —
You'll gain one
understanding
friend.

ONE MINUTE

Time is a thing that
I can't understand
Although I am living
right in it —
It's strange that the
fastest and laziest man
Are both in the
very same
minute.

ONE ROAD

So many roads spread
out for us to take.
We must choose one—
there's no alternative—
While down the other
ways we dimly see
Our other selves
who now will
never live.

ONE'S NICHE

I must not strain to
do too much,
Move mountains with
my puny will—
I'll fill with ease
and dignity
The place in life
I'm meant
to fill.

ONE WAY

One way I have to
  baffle woe
When failure follows
  all I've tried—
I suddenly detach
  myself
And just sit still and
  let things
  slide.

OPEN BOOK

I can't conceal my
  crimes.
I'm really quite
  distressed—
My life's an open
  book
That ought
  to be
  suppressed!

OPERATION

I've lost a sympathetic
friend.
She underwent an
operation —
She lived, but just to
talk about
Insides in
all her
conversation.

OPINION

What people might think
shall not govern my life
Whatever I want I
will dare.
I'm a slave to opinion
though nevertheless —
I want them to know
I don't care.

OPTIMISTS

Although I side with
optimists
And think they have
the right of it,
I'm not just glad
because of life,
But often-times
in spite
of it.

OPTION

Though the world is at
times a troublous place
And often my life seems
dull and drear
When I think I could
leave if I wanted to
I always begin to
like it here.

ORATOR

I love to talk about
myself
And bask in public
admiration—
Although I'm not so
grand in life
I'm glorified in
conversation.

ORDINARY DAYS

Weather beautifies
the world—
Rain and sun and
haze
Give a changing
loveliness
To ordinary
days.

OSTENTATION

Why do I want
 possessions
When I ought to want,
 I know,
A spacious life for
 action,
Not a cluttered one
 for show?

OSTRICH

Why guard myself
 from sorrow
And hide a coward
 head?
I might discover
 later
I'd hid from
 life instead.

OTHER SELVES

In my past I can see
a procession of selves,
They march in a glamour
not based upon fact—
From the infant in arms
to the aged and bowed
They're acting the way
I intended
to act.

OTHER SORROW

Some trouble comes
to everyone.
We're never sad
alone—
If we could think of
others' woes
We might forget
our own.

OTHERS' ADVICE

I ask advice from
others.
I seldom take it
though —
I simply let them
give it
Because they
love it so.

OUR LIVES

Our lives all
interweave,
Each needed in its
place.
And every heavy
heart
Is weighing down
the race.

OUR WORLD

The moon is a queen who
walks lovely and mute;
The sun is majestic
and golden and high,
The stars are like notes
on a heavenly flute —
But our world is the
funniest thing
in the sky.

OUTCAST

Some people seem at
ease in life.
Like fish they move
in schools —
While some like me,
don't fit at all
And never
know the
rules.

OUTDOOR MUSIC

I love the concerts
in the park —
Beneath the far and
quiet stars
I hear faint strains
of music steal
Through children's cries
and roaring
cars.

OUTGROWING FEAR

When I let my troubles
scare me
Black and huge they
look and tall —
But if I face them
full of courage
I grow big
and they
grow small.

OUT OF SEASON

The rain that rains
in the springtime
Brings violets, you
recall —
But name me one
good reason
For rain that
rains in
the fall.

OUTLOOK

We can't look far
ahead or back.
By time we're over-
awed —
Well, since my view
of life's not long
I'll try to
keep it
broad.

PAIN

The deepest joy is
felt by those
Who know what pain
is, too—
And I belong in this
large group
And so do most
of you.

PALMISTRY

A palmist read my
hand today.
It filled me with
surprise—
In spite of what
I've always thought
It seems I'm strong
and wise!

PAMPERED

Oh, why are people
cross to me
To spoil my day and
make me blue —
I'm always nice to
all of them
Who act the way I
want them to.

PANACEAS

Although I have a
frightful cold
I think I might endure
it
If all my friends
would not insist
I try their ways
to cure it.

PANGS

Oh, how I regret in
the night
With pangs that will
never abate
Those brilliantly
crushing retorts
I think of a little
too late!

PARADE

I feel that life
eludes me.
Things always move
too fast —
By the time I reach
the curbstone
The big parade
has passed.

PARDON

I pardon my enemies
gladly.
It makes me feel
noble and strong—
The thing that is
harder for me is
Forgiving the
people I
wrong.

PARTNERS

I want to tell the
world
Whenever I am glad,
For happiness
unshared
Becomes a little
sad.

PASSIONATE POET

"We suffer, who bravely
clasp life to our hearts,"
The passionate poet
exultingly cried.
For life, that the rest
of us simply accept,
He takes as a matter
of personal
pride.

THE PAST

It's solemn to think
that every night
When I fasten my
bedroom door
I am closing the door
on another day,
That I never
can enter
more.

PAST AND FUTURE

Although the future
looks so dark
And strange and still
and vast
It seems quite
natural and safe
As soon as it
is past.

PASTORAL

I long to be in the
country now
Where birds are
building in the eaves,
To hear the soft
mysterious talk
Of rain among
the budding
leaves.

PATTERNS

People's lives unwind
like ribbons,
Crisscrossed, common
with sublime,
Making strange and
colored patterns
On the grey
expanse of
Time.

PAY

I'm sorry that the
world's arranged
So we must do our
work for pay—
I always feel I
gain the most
When I can give my
work away.

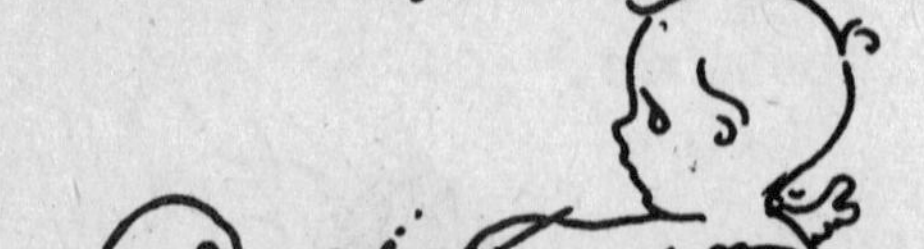

PAY DAY

Monday is the longest
day,
Saturday is filled
with glee,
Sunday has a
peaceful charm
But pay day
is the day
for me.

PEBBLES

Some people say the
whole wide world is sad
Because their own small
thoughts are cross or blue
And yet you cannot say
the road is bad
Because you have
a pebble in
your shoe.

PERFECTION

Well, since I find it
irksome
To slave for world
success
I won't neglect my
talent
For perfect laziness.

PERSPECTIVE

To concentrate on one
small worry
Makes it seem as
large as space
But when I see life
in perspective
Worries fill a little
place.

PESSIMISTS

The pessimists spread
gloom about
They always hold
such dreary views —
They should be
quarantined I think
So other folks won't
catch their
blues.

PESTS

Upon the growing list
of those
I soon shall have to
rise and slay
Are countless souls
who ask me if
It's hot enough
for me
today.

PETALS

The sun is just a
flower gay
That blooms above us
very high,
And every fragrant,
soft-aired day
A petal falling from
the sky.

PET AVERSION

My aversion to work
is so great
That when I'm at last
Forced to do it
I really work harder
than most
I hurry so fast to get
through it.

PETTINESS

When I whine of the
smallness of life,
Of monotonous days,
It is possible I am
at fault
With my small fretful
ways.

PETTY ANNOYANCES

People at movies who
sit next to me
And make witty comments
on all that they see,
And people who breathe
in my ears in the car
Had better look out—
I'll be tried
just so far!

PHILANTHROPISTS

Among my pet
aversions
Are people who
expand
In a luxury of pity
As they lend
a helping
hand.

PHILOSOPHY

Each strange and new
philosophy
I studied hopefully in
youth.
That every man must
stand alone
Is all I've ever
learned
of truth.

PHOTOGRAPHS

I'm thankful for
photographers,
As age creeps on
apace,
Who take those misty
photographs
That hide the well-
worn face.

PICKLES

Though life has bitter
little times
They're not a total
loss I feel
For mixed with joys
they play the part
Of sour pickles
at a meal.

PICNIC

I like to picnic in
the woods.
It broadens me I
find —
It's one time I can
eat an ant
And really hardly
mind.

PIONEER

To live my life
convention-bound
I never could be
willing —
Untraveled roads are
often rough
But then
they're always
thrilling.

PIRATES

Conversational pirates
Have caused me many
a groan—
They hear a
witticism
And use it as their
own.

PLAINTIVE

I met a deadly
bore today.
I thought I'd never
get away.
You wouldn't hear
this loud complaining
If she had found <u>me</u>
entertaining.

PLAN

We're all a part of one
big plan
To work together,
not compete —
Thus one who beats
his fellow man
Has really caused his
own defeat.

PLANETARY THOUGHT

Clear and far shines
a star,
A lovely steadfast
light —
Perhaps our world is
shining too
In some star-dweller's
sight.

PLANETS

When stars fill the sky,
Shining steadfast
and far,
How lovely to think
That we live on
a star!

PLAYTHING

Sometimes I feel so
powerful,
A lovely mood to start
the day with —
As if the world is
just a ball
That God has
given me to
play with.

PLUGGING

If life could be all
crises
I'd live with zest
and glee —
It's just this steady
plugging
That gets
the best
of me.

POETS

The poets talk like
supermen
In strange, uplifting verse.
But when you meet
them you can see
They're just the same as
you and me,
Or sometimes
even worse.

POET'S DREAM

Not more pathetic is
the bud
Untimely nipped by
March's blight
Than youthful poets'
tender verse
That never blooms
in black
and white.

POINT OF VIEW

Sometimes in light and
idle chatter
A careless unkind
word I say—
And yet it seems a
serious matter
If people speak of me
that way.

POLISH

I have a bottle of old
red glass.
I have a little smooth
silver gazelle.
Time has polished them,
flowing past,
As waves polish pebbles
and bits
of shell.

POLITENESS

Now animals aren't
polite,
Each tries to outdo
his own brother,
But we tip our hats
when we meet
And open the
door for
each other.

POMP

Fate has played me
  lots of tricks,
Some tragic, some
  absurd,
As when I make a
  pompous speech,
And mispronounce
  a word.

POOL

I can't roam freely
  through the world,
Life seems to shut
  me in with bars;
And yet a pool that
  lies quite still
Can mirror flying birds
  and stars.

POOR FISH

Fish seem so
indignant
With rude, unseeing
stare —
I'm glad they live in
water
And not just
everywhere.

POSE

It's not to gain some
lofty end
I heed ambition's
call —
It's just to show the
world, alas,
I labor,
if at all.

POSSESSIONS

Possessions weigh me
down in life.
I never feel quite free.
I wonder if I own
my things
Or if my things
own me.

POSTMAN

Although I see him
every day
With hope and joy my
poor heart bounds.
And yet I've never
heard his name—
He's just the
postman on
his rounds.

I'd love to be a
  traffic cop
And tell the world to
  go or stop,
Or in an office boy's
  proud place
Take down a peg the
  human race.

POWER OF SILENCE

The power of words
  is great.
It can move the
  stubbornest will—
But sometimes I envy
  more
The power of
  keeping still.

PRACTISE

My days are full of
blunders —
Oh, how I've always
yearned
To live one life for
practise,
Another when
I've learned!

PRAYER

May I walk my ways
Clear-eyed and
free
And do some good
Anonymously.

PREFERENCE

I much prefer a
person
With a black heart
underneath
To some pure soul who
sniffles
Or whistles
through his
teeth.

PRESENT

This moment is the
peak of time.
On it we stand and
we can see
The future and the
past stretch out,
Two roads
to one
eternity.

PRESIDENT

I wonder if the
  president
Has family spats
  and jokes,
And eats green onions
  in the spring
Just like us common
  folks.

PRETENSION

Most all the money
  that I earn
By truly superhuman
  labors
Goes not for things
  for which I yearn
But just for
 things to show
 my neighbors.

PRIDE

I threw my coat
  around me
To take a haughty
  leave,
But my hand went
  through the lining
Instead of
  down the
  sleeve!

PRIMAVERA

Tapestries of sight
  and sound
The lovely springtime
  weaves,
With crystal beads of
  birdsong strews
The lacy
  green of
  leaves.

PRIZE

People are blind who
strive too hard
To climb to some prize
above —
The simplest thing in
the world is joy,
And the nearest thing
is love.

PROBLEM

Deciding a problem is
harder for me
Than to act when I've
made a decision.
"Well, would you, or
wouldn't you, or would
you?" I ask
Till my friends
howl me down
in derision.

PROCESSION

Down the years in
grand procession
Poets march with
deathless song,
While with countless
little verses
Stubbornly I
tag along.

PROCRASTINATION

Always put off till
tomorrow
The worry that
threatens today,
Because you may find
when that time comes
The reason has
vanished away.

PROGRESS

In my youth I set
my goal
Farther than the eye
could see.
I am nearer to it
now —
I have moved
it nearer me.

PROPORTION

When I was small
the world I knew
Was safe and far
from vast —
It seems to me that
as I grew
The world grew
twice as
fast.

PROSPERITY

In moments of
depression
I never get so low
But once I reach
the bottom,
Rebounding,
up I go.

PUBLICITY

Gossip shall not cramp
my life.
Boldly through the
world I'll walk —
I'd rather far be
talked about
Than one of
those who
merely talk.

PUDDLES

In deep and almost
liquid mud
I dropped my only
dime.
I didn't find it —
but I searched
And had a
lovely time.

PULL

If I should get ahead
through pull
Instead of earning
my advance
I'd lose as much in
character
As I'd be gaining
in finance.

PURSUIT

I must go north in
summer time.
In winter for the
south I'm bound.
I cannot settle down
to live—
The weather
chases me
around.

PUZZLES

If I should spend in
working
The intellect and
care
I use on cross word
puzzles
I'd be a
millionaire.

QUANDARY

Two questions ask
yourself
When worries cloud
your brow:
Is it something I can
help,
And can I help it now?

QUARREL

To keep up a quarrel
Is simply absurd
For nobody ever
Has said the last
word.

Q

QUERY

They say a life of
struggle grim,
Of facing every
task,
Will get you some
place in the end —
But where,
if I may
ask?

QUEST

Where do the flies go
in winter
When the cold winds
come blowing again?
And a question that
bothers me more is:
What becomes of the
hand-organ
men?

QUESTION

?

There's a question that's
always in my mind;
It bothers me and will
not cease —
Is it better to be a
grabby child
Or always take the
smallest
piece?

QUIET

When I have sternly
judged my friends
As I am moved to do
at times
I'm so embarrassed
afterwards
To contemplate my own
great crimes.

Across the moonlight
on the snow
I saw a young, wild
rabbit go
How lightly!—making
no more sound
Than his long
shadow on
the ground.

RADICAL VIEWS

I really hold radical
views about life.
Convention bars progress
I very well know.
I always decide things
with untrammeled mind—
I'm too nice to
live up to my
principles
though.

RADIO

How fast words go
by radio!
For miles the speaker's
loud voice reaches—
A great improvement
this might be
If only they'd improve
the speeches.

RADIO CURE

How strange would be
the radio
If people talking
through it
Could run around and
hear themselves—
But, no, they cannot
do it.

RAINBOW

A pot of gold you're
  sure to find
If to the rainbow's
  end you go —
The man who has a
  pot of gold
Can't always find
  a rainbow
  though.

RAIN OR SHINE

When days are much
  too cold or hot
We talk about it
  hours together —
It's funny how the
  human race
Will sort of
  brag about
  the weather.

RAIN SONG

The rain goes rushing
down the street.
Soft gusts of sound
it utters.
It sings a spring song
cool and sweet
And chuckles in
the gutters.

RARE BIRD

Is there one among
all my young readers
Who ever has heard
a faint rumor
Of a person who
claimed a low instep,
Or said he had
no sense
of humor?

RARE FRIENDS

Why are true friends
so rare
I ask with mournful
sigh —
I ought to ask
instead:
What kind
of friend
am I?

READING

Reading is my
greatest joy.
Its pleasures never
pale —
My favorite form
of literature
Is ads of farms
for sale.

REALITY

One-sided is a life
all joy
For sorrow also
plays a part —
I want to welcome
everything
That brings
life closer
to my heart.

REAL POETS

The poets writing
deathless verse
Must almost give
their work away—
I wish that I wrote
poetry
So lovely that it
didn't pay.

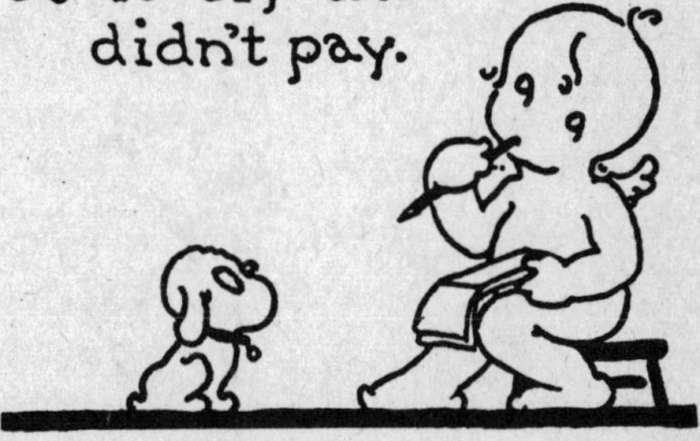

REAL WOE

There's not a person
in the world
Who hasn't had some
woe.
Why is it mine seems
much more real
Than other people's
though?

REASON

At times life seems all
struggle and confusion,
But don't forget another
world is near:
The world of thought that
we can always enter
Where everything is
reasoned, calm
and clear.

REBIRTH

Never let past
bitterness
Make you cynical
today.
Each dawn the world
is born anew—
Let your heart
be born
that way.

RECIPROCATION

Look on things with
friendly eyes,
Cast out little hates.
Just love life with
all your heart—
Life reciprocates.

RECOLLECTION

The joys I've had and
  lost
Don't cause me much
  regret —
The joys that might
  have been
Are those I
  can't forget.

RECOMPENSE

Virtue is its own
  reward,
But just to make life
  pleasant
When I've been good
  or labored hard
I buy myself
  a present.

REFLECTION

Sometimes I see my life
with such calm eyes
Withdrawn and far
beyond,
The way the moon looks
down and sees a moon
Wave-broken
on a pond.

REFORM

I like myself the
way I am.
Of faults I've more
than one.
If anyone reformed
me though
I'd miss
a lot
of fun.

REGRET

Through fear of taking
risks in life
I've missed a lot of
fun—
The only things that
I regret
Are those I haven't
done.

REJECTION

I send out poems
every mail
But back they come—
they never fail.
The postman rings my
bell each day—
Well, that is
something
anyway.

REJUVENATION

When I long for a change
  and can't travel
There are plenty of
  things I can do
Such as getting a new
  kind of haircut
Or even a new
  point of view.

RELATIVE

I ought to judge my
  neighbors' deeds
With never-failing
  charity —
My own intentions and
  my acts
Show such a great
  disparity.

Life extends on either
side
Much farther than the
eye can see —
How strange that I
should concentrate
So wholly on
what comes
to me!

RELAXATION

Things will snap when
stretched too tight,
So why be nervous
and intense?
I'll just relax, and
laughingly
And limberly
I'll meet
events.

RELIEF

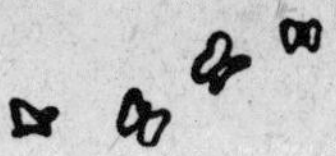

After thunder storms
are done
All the world seems
fresh and glad.
That's the way I
sometimes feel
After getting
good and
mad.

REMEMBERING

I am told I shouldn't
worry,
I am told I shouldn't
fret —
So I'm trying to
remember
All the things
I must
forget.

REMINISCENCE

When I was little there
were hitching posts
Of horses' heads or
little iron boys
All down the street; and
when I went for walks
I clanked their
rings and made
a lovely noise.

REMORSE

It's not the wicked
life I've lived
That makes me shed
this tear —
It's all the life I've
simply lost
Through laziness
or fear.

RENDEZVOUS

Reader, far away from
me,
Whom I'll never know
or see,
It's strange through
just this printed line
Our thoughts are
meeting, yours
and mine.

RENUNCIATIONS

To cling too hard to
joy
Is far from wise
I know —
It takes a lot more
strength
At times to
let it go.

REPENTANCE

I like to feel repentant
when
I haven't done the
things I should—
It makes me feel
more virtuous
Than if I'd kept on
being good!

RESIGNATION

It's foolish fighting
sorrow
With struggles, cries
and tears,
For when we just
accept it
It almost
disappears.

RESOLUTION

I've made new rules
this New Year's —
I realize at times
I've got to have
more system
If only in my
crimes!

RESOLVE

I let the blues creep
in today —
I'll take possession
of tomorrow
And cram it full of
work and play
And not leave any
room for
sorrow.

Be lazy sometimes, I
advise.
Don't blame yourself
and think you shirk.
It's very wise to
realize
That resting is a part
of work.

RESTLESS

Through the muffling
fog
I hear the steam
boat's call,
And long to go,
but where
I do not know
at all.

REVELATION

I lose illusions one by
one
And see beneath the
surface glitter;
But though it's sometimes
quite a shock
The truth should
never make
me bitter.

REVENGE

Tomorrow I'll get
even
With all those friends
so dear
Who gave me gilded
shoe trees.
And things
like that
last year.

REVOLVING DOORS

Revolving doors are
spiteful things
I cannot help but
feel.
Unless I leap out
breathlessly,
They nip me
on the
heel.

REWARD

Never ask for joy.
Do the day's small
task
The very best you
can—
Joy will come
unasked.

RHYTHM

I'm writing this verse
by some apple trees
Midst grumbling and
scolding wasps and bees,
While ants course over
me mile on mile
Destroying my usual
rhythmical
style.

RICHES

I'd be a whole lot
richer
Than millionaires
and kings
If I wanted not more
money
But rather fewer
things.

RIPE

The joys of youth
may leave me.
I'll worry not at all.
For though I like
the summer
My favorite time
is fall.

RISKS

Don't run from risks
that block your path.
Just take them in
your stride—
The only refuge
really safe
Is on the
other side.

ROADWAYS

When cold and dismal
  is the dawn
And days are dark
  and drear
I like to think of all
  the roads
That lead away
  from here.

ROAMING

I love it when I first
  wake up
These springtime
  mornings gold and blue,
And see the spacious
  sunny day
Spread out for me,
  to wander
  through.

ROGUE

I should be always
good and kind
With heart of gold
and manners nice
But charming people
seem to have
A little wickedness,
for spice:

RÔLE

No one would guess from
my humble attire
And plain, ineffectual
face
That really within I'm
a creature of fire
And full of
high courage
and grace.

O Fate, if you must
pick on me
Pray heed my
exhortations
And send me woes of
dignity,
Not countless
irritations.

ROMANCE

I wonder if everyone
else
Sees his life as a
marvelous story,
And walks through
monotonous days
In a cloud
of invisible
glory.

ROUND TRIP

I'm sorry that the
 world is round—
It sometimes makes me
 sad at heart
To think my longest
 journey here
Will bring me
 back to
where I
 start.

ROUTINE

Of washing, dressing,
 work and meals
My frantic days
 consist.
I hardly live at all—
 it's such
A labor to
 exist.

RUEFUL

The secret sorrows that
  I nurse
And never can confide
Are not my tragic
  ones — they're worse —
They're those that
  hurt my
    pride.

RULES

Conventions cramp my
  sweeping style.
Why should I be
  ruled by custom?
Rules were only
  made, I think,
For those
  who are too
  weak to
    bust 'em.

SAD MOODS

Without a reason now
and then
Sad moods come
settling down on men,
And no one can escape
them, so
Don't fight them and
they soon
will go.

SANCTUARY

I'm forced to be
courageous
When in danger or
despair —
I try to run for
shelter
But the shelter
isn't there.

SATISFACTION

The least little thing
makes me happy today
In my mood of
unreasoning glee—
Oh my, but I'm glad that
I'm nobody else,
Because it's
such fun
to be me!

SCENERY

I love our mountains
in the west,
So still and strange
and tall.
I brag about our
scenery—
You'd think
I made
it all.

SCISSORS

I shed my small
possessions so
I lose things every
single day.
For instance — have you
noticed too
How scissors
simply melt
away?

SEA GULLS

The sea gulls grey
against the sky
Wheel and slant on
rigid wings.
I love their wild and
hungry cry
Much more than
songs a tame
bird sings.

SEASON'S CHANGE

I've lived with weather
all my life
It seems there's nothing
else to do—
And yet it's one thing
in the world
I cannot get
accustomed to.

SECRETS

When people tell me
secrets
I'm often moved to
ask
Since they themselves
can't keep them
Why give to me
that task.

SECRET SORROW

How little anybody
knows
Of other people's
secret woes!
How kind this ought to
make me be
To everyone,
and them
to me!

SEEING CLEAR

Our own gloomy
thoughts
Make life gloomy
too,
Just as dust in the
eyes
Can spoil a
fine view.

SEEKER

Some seek afar for
 happiness
When, if they only
 knew it,
This rule alone brings
 lasting joy —
Just find your work,
 and do it.

SELF-CENTERED

Though I'm constantly
 railing at bores
It dawned on me only
 today
That nothing I think of
 myself
Seems too unimportant
 to say!

I give advice freely
In words quick and
breezy
But when some one
takes it
I feel quite uneasy.

SELF-ESTEEM

The men whose wisdom
I esteem,
Whose words I rate
most high,
Are nearly always
just the ones
Who think the same
as I.

SELF-FORGIVENESS

I'm full of toleration
And sweet forgiveness
too
For all the many
wicked
And foolish things
I do.

SELFISH JOY

I lost my little
selfish joy
And only then did I
divine
That freely mingling
with the world
I'd gain the whole
world's joy
for mine.

SELF-PITY

I hate to be pitied
by friends
Yet at times, though
it passes belief,
I pity myself to the
point
Of almost enjoying
my grief.

SELF-RELIANCE

I've had to stay
alone for days.
However I am not
complaining—
I never realized
before
That I could be so
entertaining.

SELF-RESPECT

To keep my honest
self-respect
Is all I ever need
to do
Because it stands to
reason then
I'll have respect
from others
too.

SELF-SUFFICIENCY

Although I want a lot
of friends
(I rather like my
fellow men)
I'll be complete
within myself—
No treachery can
hurt me
then.

SENSE OF HUMOR

Although I suffer tragic
woe
And weep and wail and
almost die
In one small corner of
my mind
I laugh a little
on the sly.

SENSITIVE SOUL

I have for a friend such
a sensitive soul
The least little slight
makes her blue.
It gives her a chance
though to pity herself
And that's what she
likes best
to do.

SENTIMENTALITY

I dont like sentimental
friends —
Afraid to wound each
tender heart
I'm forced, though
inwardly I rage,
To act a
sentimental
part.

SERENITY

Clothes and houses
hold our lives
And often we're so
blind
We never see that
life itself
Unfolds within
the mind.

I think uplifting
thoughts at times
And straightway put
them into rhymes—
It's much more difficult
I know
To put them into
practise though.

SERVICE

We demand perfect
service wherever we go.
We're enraged at the
slightest neglect—
But consider the poor
human race as it is
And it seems
quite a lot
to expect.

Shadows in the noon-
day sun are sharp;
At sunset they are long
and soft and still.
So troubles that are black
and hard in youth
Grow soft with age—
at least I think
they will.

SHAME

Though kind and proper
I appear
It often gives me
quite a jar
To look beneath my
gentle acts
And fathom what my
motives are!

SHAPES

While animals live
care-free lives
And birds soar high on
joyous wings
The human race with
wood and nails
Just fills the world
with shapes
of things.

SHELTER

With little strict
conventions
And formal words
and acts
We build ourselves a
shelter
From life's most
sweeping
facts.

SHOCKING

It's strange that an
  earthquake,
Far distant though
  shocking,
Disturbs me much
  less than
A run in my
  stocking!

SHOPPING

It takes all the joy from
  a wild shopping spree
And the next day it
  drives me distraught
To find that the shops
  took me seriously
And sent me
  the things
  that I
  bought!

SHOW

If you think that the
world is all wrong,
That civilization's a
botch,
At least you will have
to admit
It's a pretty good
show to
watch.

SHOWERS

I long to run through
the summer rain,
To lift my face when
the big drops fall
And lie and laugh in
the cool wet grass
With hardly
anything
on at all.

SHRINKING

Little drops of water,
Little grains of sand
It seems my stylish
bathing suit
Was never meant
to stand.

SICK-A-BED

It's sympathy I
want when ill.
With rage I almost
yell
To have friends
say, "Well, anyway,
You're *looking* very
well."

SILENCE

Beyond this noise I
love to think
The sky is filled
with silence vast
That closes in behind
our world
When once it
whizzes
loudly past.

SILENT MUSIC

Unhurried, soft, the
soundless snow
Falls gently to the
frozen ground—
Such perfect stillness
sometimes seems
More musical
than any
sound.

SILVER LINING

It's never wise to
wail too soon.
Misfortunes always
end—
The day that brought
my deepest woe
Brought too my
truest friend.

SILVER RAINS

The rain that falls in
silver lines
Makes everywhere a
soft vague sound,
Connecting silent far-off
clouds
With clouds
of music
on the ground.

I'd like to live a
simple life
And concentrate on
some high aim
Ignoring worldly
pomp and show,
If all my friends
would do
the same.

SIMPLE PLEASURES

I like to walk fences
And eke roll down
hills —
At such simple
pleasures
My simple
heart thrills.

Although I've quite
enjoyed my sins
They bother me at
times —
Oh, how I wish that
I might have
The courage
of my
crimes!

SKIPPING-ROPES

With marbles, jacks and
skipping ropes
Every spring the
children play,
Keeping still alive the
games
That you and
I played
years away.

SKY

I love the tender
brooding sky,
It rests my eyes
and spirit too—
I wish that I could
climb up high
And plunge my
arms deep
in its blue.

SLEEP

The night makes
people more united.
While awake they're
far asunder,
But sleep is like a
warm, grey blanket
All of us can huddle
under.

SLOTH

Of course I'd prefer
to be wealthy
But rather than slave
to excess
I'll be just a leisurely
failure
Instead of
a dismal
success.

SMALL AMBITIONS

Why should I yearn
for honors great?
Enough for me my
work well done.
How often thus I
meditate
And scorn the fame
I've never
won!

SMALL TALK

From the first day
that weather began
We've been never a
minute without it —
And there's never a
minute as well
When no one
is talking
about it!

SMALL THINGS

I love small uncivilized
things,
Babies and rabbits
and birds,
Who carry around
in their eyes
Little strange
thoughts
without words.

SMART ALECK

Whenever I have been
unkind
To say a thing that's
smart,
Although it stimulates
my mind
It later hurts
my heart.

SMILES

Age has the lightest
touch
Upon the kind of face
Where ghosts of
many smiles
Have left a gentle
trace.

SMUGNESS

I feel so smug when
I've been good
I soon become
unbearable —
I'm really pleasanter
to know
When I have just been
terrible!

SNAPSHOTS

I hate to look at
pictures of myself.
I hold them yards away
and squint my eyes,
And yet they show a
most disastrous face —
I won't believe
the camera
never lies.

SNEERS

Only stupid people
sneer —
The man who has
an open mind
Can understand the
world's mistakes
And, understanding them,
be kind.

SNOW

When I was little I
welcomed the snow
To coast on or wade in
or simply to throw.
Oh, how I hope when I'm
solemn and old
I'll never
complain of
the snow and
the cold!

SOARING THOUGHTS

No matter where my
body moves
My shadow follows me
around
But thoughts I think
can soar like birds
That leave
their shadows
on the ground.

SOCIAL AMENITIES

I've told my last
polite white lie.
My pleasant smile
is numb.
When next I'm asked
to tea I'll say
"No, thanks,
I'd hate
to come."

SOCIAL CALLS

When pleasures pall
upon my mind
And social calls I
shirk,
In fact when I am
bored I find
It rests me
some to
work.

SOCIAL LAW

Why can't we introduce
ourselves
To people on the
street?
I know I pass a lot
of friends
I'll never get
to meet.

SOCIAL SUCCESS

I might be a social
success
Instead of unknown
and ignored,
Except for one defect
in me —
I cannot endure
being bored.

SOLO

I wish I could sing
when I'm happy.
I try but my efforts
are vain —
It's queer when I'm
feeling so blissful
To sound like
a person
in pain.

SOLUTION

I had a problem in
my life.
I pondered on it
filled with care.
But once I'd gathered
all the facts
I saw the problem
wasn't there.

SOMETHING NICE

When life is just a
dreary grind
And friends seem
fated to annoy,
Say something nice to
some one else
And watch the world
light up
with joy.

SORROW

You have to be worthy
of sorrow.
Sorrow is deep and
true.
When life makes a
chord like music
Sorrow is in it
too.

SOULS

Through war and
suffering and woe
To ever distant goals
All bravely forging
on alone
We steer our little
souls.

SOURCE OF SORROW

Whenever I am gloomy
In time I come
to see
It's just because
I'm thinking
Entirely of me.

SOUTHERN SEAS

By seeking summer
out of turn
Along some southern
sea
I'd miss the thrill of
shy sweet spring
Who now comes
seeking me.

Trees are lovely in a
breeze.
They make a soft
contented sound,
And gracefully their
moving limbs
Toss flakes of
shadow on
the ground.

SPACE

The world is wide;
on every side
New wonders we can
find—
And yet for each man
space extends
No farther than
his mind.

SPANGLES

Like spangles on the
fabric
Of daily work and
duty
Are countless little
moments
Of evanescent
beauty.

SPEECHLESS

At times when callers
fill the room
A heavy silence falls
like doom,
And helplessly I
wonder then,
"Will no one ever
speak again?"

When friends accuse
me of my crimes
I candidly confess
they're true —
For this exasperates
them more
Than anything that
I could do.

SPLASH

I love goloshes and
slickers so,
Their names sort of
splash together.
I flop and slip through
the sloppy snow —
Oh, how I
enjoy bad
weather!

SPORT

I'll try to take the
blows of fate
With robust strength
and glee,
And simply laugh and
say, "All right —
This time
the joke's
on me."

SPOTLIGHT

Although I'm really
far from well
I feel no apprehension.
It's one sure way
that I can be
The center of
attention.

It feels like spring
all over the world.
I cannot believe at all
That on different parts
of the earth right now
Are winter and summer
and fall.

SPRING FEVER

Out must I gallop
from the house
And gambol on the lea,
For spring has come
to field and wood
And most of all
to me!

STAMPS

With all my hard-
earned cash
Most recklessly I
part
But when I waste
a stamp
It simply
breaks my
heart.

STAR

A star was shining in
a well.
I let the pail down
slow and far.
It broke the light to
little bits —
But once I
almost had
a star!

STARRY CRYSTALS

Winter is the time
of stars—
Not only in the sky
they glow
But millions of them
crystal clear,
Are all around
us in the
snow.

STATEMENTS

Neat and orderly
am I—
I clean my desk out
now and then
And gaze on piles of
notes and bills
And throw them all
back in
again.

STATESMEN

Statesmen stand in
long black coats
And speak wise words
from ample throats.
I always think with
wonder then
Of how small babes
become
such men!

STATUE

I love a statue old
and still.
Ancient moods pervade
it.
It's strange how much
more real it is
Than the hand
that made it.

STICK-TO-IT-IVENESS

A clever idea's like a
snowball, I think.
Push it, it surely
will grow.
But nothing will come of
the weightiest thought
If you think it and
let it go.

STOIC

I wish when losses
came to me
I bore them calmly,
like a tree
That stands up proud
against the sky
And sheds its
leaves without
a sigh.

STONE

I'd like to buy a
diamond ring—
I pay my board
instead.
Alas, I ask of life
a stone
And all I get
is bread!

STORMS

I'd like to take my
grief the way
A tree bends to the
storms that beat it
To see it as a part
of life
And, by accepting it,
defeat it.

STRANGER

I'm so penned up
inside myself
I'd like to step away
And see me as a
stranger would
Who met me
just today.

STREAM OF LIFE

The stream of life
flows darkly
Its strange deep ways
along,
But on its waves are
bubbles
Of rainbow
mirth and
song.

STREET SOUNDS

I love to hear the
 wind blow by
With sounds that rise
 and fall and die,
And then the rain
 rush down the street
Upon its million
 quick grey
 feet.

STRENGTH

Life cannot hurt the
 adventurous soul
Who meets it with
 head proudly high.
Only the timid are
 beaten by fate
For life simply
 passes
 them by.

STRONG CHARACTERS

Strong characters are
noble
But with rage it
makes me squirm
To see them acting
stubborn
When they
think they're
being firm.

STUBBORN

The whole world
changes every day.
Why, even mountains
wear away.
And yet at times I
lag behind
And boast, "I never
change my
mind!"

STUDY

We study a trade or
profession for years
Before we can hope
for success —
And yet though we want
to have lives full of joy
We all study living
much less.

STYLE

I've lost some great
and stylish friends
I'm glad as I can be
The strain of living
up to them
Was nearly killing
me.

SUBTLE JOYS

My praise of simple
homely joys
Is sometimes over-
stated —
I often yearn, I
must admit,
For joys more
complicated.

SUBTLETY

When I want to
flatter people
And to make them
think I'm nice
I have found the
surest method
Is to ask them for
advice.

SUCCESS

To get ahead is not
success.
Progressive men, I
often find,
Have hurried so for
worldly wealth
That they have left
their souls
behind.

SUMMER

The summer sun is like
a bird—
Around the spacious
sky it swings,
And down float light
and shining days
Like golden feathers
from its
wings.

The different days
  that circle round
The small and
  patient earth
Are dark because the
  sun has frowned
Or sunny
  with his
  mirth.

SUN AND MOON

The sun helps farmers
  grow their grain.
It's patient, strong
  and slow —
The moon shines down
  in poets' eyes
And little verses
  grow.

SUN BATH

I dream of garments
soft as mist
And light as moonbeams
on the sea—
I got so sunburned
yesterday
That nothing
else will
do for me.

SUNBURNED

So redly am I sun-
burned
Like roast beef
under-done
The beet is pale
beside me
And wan the
setting sun.

SUNDAY AFTERNOONS

I hate to go for dusty
rides
On every Sunday
afternoon
And have to talk to
silly friends
Until at last
I simply
swoon.

SUNDAY BLUES

I can spend six days
a week
In solitude and never
moan,
But Sunday evening
is a time
When <u>no</u> one ought to
be alone.

SUN MAGIC

The great all-seeing
sun shines down
And searches out the
smallest things,
Turns spider webs to
threads of gold,
Makes high lights on
the beetle's
wings.

SUNNY DAYS

I can't feel sad or
care at all
About my lack of
money
When skies are blue
and trees are green
And days are long
and sunny.

To skim the surface of
the day
Is foolish, wasteful,
blind,
For every minute has
a heart
That I must
try to
find.

SUPER-FRIENDS

Where are those
faultless people,
So brilliant, gay and
kind —
Those super-friends
we dream of
And somehow
never find.

SUPPRESSION

The sharp retort I
  didn't say
Has lightened some
  one's load.
I must be gentle
  every day —
At least,
 till I
 explode!

SURROUNDINGS

I wish I had a
  different house,
With slides instead
  of stairs
And springboards on
  the landings too
And cushions
  everywheres.

We like a winding
road the best.
By each new view
we're onward led—
So half the charm of
life is this:
We cannot see
too far
ahead.

SUSPICION

Suspicion builds a wall
around our hearts,
And cautiously we guard
our little pride,
Not seeing, foolish mortals,
that the wall
Is worse than any hurt
it keeps
outside.

SWALLOWS

I love to watch the
  swallows soar.
With lilting rhythmic
  grace they fly,
As if a flock of small
  black notes
Were writing
  music on
  the sky.

SWEEPING

I like to sweep the
  front porch steps;
The sun shines and the
  birds all sing.
I hate to sweep the
  kitchen floor —
I never see
  or hear
  a thing.

SWEET TEA

I hate those sweetly
simpering moods
That just possess me
at a tea—
I feel that helplessly
I act
Like some one else
burlesquing me.

SYMPHONY

Each little bug so
unconcerned
Contributes chirpingly
his song
To make that vast
and cheerful sound
That sweeps the earth
all summer long.

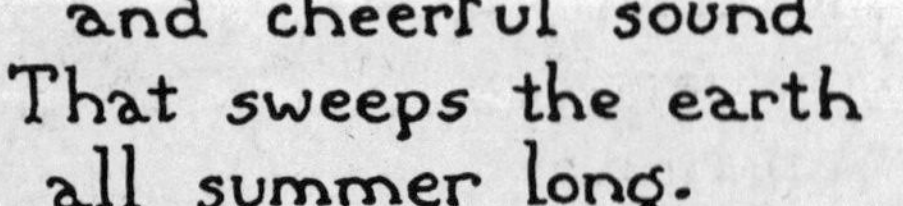

TACT

When you've made an
awful blunder
Don't bewail your
brainless act —
Think of all your past
successes,
Show yourself a
little tact.

TACTLESSNESS

The moon is kind to
lovers,
None friendlier than
she —
But to the lonely-
hearted
How tactless
she can be!

TAKING CHANCES

I'll always take risks to
do things that I want.
Although the results may
be bad
I'm willing to suffer—
at least I can feel
I'm paying for
something
I've had.

TALENT

I'll never have the
Fortune
Which only genius
brings
But I have a lot of
talent
For enjoying little
things.

TALK

People live their lives
  in crowds.
They talk and talk
  without control—
But each one sees
  himself at heart
A strong and
  solitary soul.

TALKERS

The past is like a
  fading cloud—
We huddle on the
  future's brink,
Surrounded by
  eternity,
And tell each other
  what we think.

TARGET

I pounded my finger
  instead of the nail,
Though I aimed, I am
  sure, at its head.
The next time I try I'll
  succeed without fail—
I'll aim at
  my finger
  instead.

TEACHER

Lives of great men all
  remind us
When we see their
  pictured features
Few of them in looks
  are greater
Than the humblest
  of God's
  creatures.

TEAMWORK

Be proud when you do
a thing well
No matter how humble
your place,
For it's pretty good
teamwork at that,
To help on
the whole
human race.

TEARS

It helps at times to
have a cry.
The sooner then your
grief is past.
So better weep and
wail say I
Than hoard
your woe and
make it last.

TEARS IDLE TEARS

I think of woes I
  might have had
At night until I
  cannot sleep,
And feel so sorry for
  myself
I'm really almost moved
  to weep.

TELLTALE

It's not my many
  foolish deeds
On which I sadly
  brood—
What's worse is that
  I tell them all
In some expansive
  mood.

TEMPER

I'm nearly always
calm and mild.
My temper very rarely
breaks —
But now and then in
rages wild
I blame the
world for
my mistakes.

THANKSGIVING

I'm filled with gratitude
today
Though dark and
drear the sky,
Because I'm filled with
turkey too
And also
pumpkin pie.

THAWS

The spring that melts
  the snow
And frees the frozen
  streams
Melts too my winter's
  woe
And helps me grow
  new dreams.

THEATRE

Just before a thunder
  storm
The outdoors has a
  yellow glow,
Unreal and so theatrical
I feel like some one
  in a show.

THEORY

I study new philosophies
But always feel when-
e'er I read them
They cannot help me
if I'm weak
And if I'm strong
I'll never
need them.

THERMOMETER

I moan about the
heat
And wish that it
would go—
I feel a sort of pride
When it breaks
a record
though.

THINGS

Things to do and
things to own
Make my life a
hampered race —
I often think that all
I want
Is just a
little time
and space.

THORNS

"Every rose has
thorns,"
Reports some keen
observer.
"Reverse that sad
remark!"
I cry with
equal fervor.

THOUGHT

My life goes on within
my mind
So I can take what
each day brings
Unhurt, when I can
realize
That life itself
is thought,
not things.

THOUGHTS OF LIFE

No sudden disaster can
damage me much
If only I'm able
to see
That I really live more
in my thoughts about life
Than just in
what happens
to me.

THRIFT

I'll never work too
long or hard—
I think it would be
funny
Since life is worth
so much to me
To spend it all for
money.

THRILL

I went out to a well
one night.
Soft darkness hid
all daytime scars.
I held some water to
the light
And drank a
dipper full
of stars.

TIDINESS

With pride I'd live
my humble life
And feel that I had
made my mark
If I could make my
fellow men
Stop throwing
papers in
the park.

TIME

Time is such a
mystery,
So gentle and so
healing —
The days slip past
like colored cards
That Father Time
is dealing.

TIME-OUT-OF-MIND

These times are out of
  joint, they cry.
The good old days
  were best they say.
And maybe even you
  and I
In fifty years
  will talk
  that way.

TIME PASSES

Each year seems shorter
  than the last.
The days and weeks
  just flicker past,
As winter, summer,
  spring and fall
Go streaking 'round
  this rolling
  ball.

TIMID SOUL

Although I live a
  blameless life
(I'm good as I can be)
I always feel so
  guilty when
Policemen look at me!

TOLERANCE

I sternly judge my
  fellow men
When I've been
  righteous for a while—
But when I've not,
  broad-mindedly
I give their faults
  a tolerant
  smile.

TAME

My youthful views were
free and wild
But, though they stay
the same,
Still younger, wilder
grows the world
And makes me feel
quite tame.

TOMORROW

Cheerily my way
I go.
To sorrow I'm
inured.
I had it once and
now I know
Tomorrow it
is cured.

TOUCH

I like the surfaces of
things,
Of leather, fur and
polished wood—
Although it's just a
minor joy
They make my fingers
feel so
good.

TOWER CLOCK

The clock in the tower
tolls
A hard and relentless
sound,
As if it would shatter
time
And fling it
upon the
ground.

The riveter's metallic song
Is like the locust's, hot
and long.
A large fat cricket is
the cop
Who chirps at cars to
go or stop—
Thus in the city
I can play
I'm in the country
anyway.

TRADE

Any job in all the
world
I'd trade mine for
today,
And I suppose that
you as well
Are feeling just
this way.

TRADING PROBLEMS

I'm free with advice
to my friends.
With a word I dissolve
all their cares—
I might be successful
myself
Could I trade my own
problems
for theirs.

TRAFFIC COPS

We thwart each other
needlessly
We're all so set on
different goals—
It might be quite a
help to us
To have some
traffic cops
for souls.

TRAVEL

Though travel is
confusing
With burdens far from
light,
By simply looking
helpless
I get along
all right.

TREASURE

Each common day has
moments we can treasure:
A laugh, a lovely sight,
a friendly speech.
They're like those gold-
flecked pebbles we discover
Among the dull grey
pebbles on
the beach.

TREE

I think I'd like to be a
 tree,
And stand and sway
 without a care;
And have the fragrant
 rain-washed wind
Run long, strong
 fingers
through my
 hair.

TRICK

I know a man who
 knows a trick —
It takes some skill
 to play it —
He always reaches
 for the check
But never
 seems to
 pay it.

TRIED AND TRUE

Sorrow comes to
everyone.
We all must struggle
through.
The things that last
through sorrow's test
Are real and
tried and
true.

TRIMMING

The fabric of my life
is grey —
Hard work in one
small place.
I'll concentrate on
trimming it
With lots of laughs
for lace.

TROLLEYS

Street cars in the
city screech,
Complaining that their
life is wrong,
But in the country
they are glad
And simply hum
and race
along.

TROUBLE

Trouble brings us
close to life.
We're stronger for the
woes we bear—
I really think I pity
those
Who never have a
single care.

TRUE FRIENDS

Although I oft bewail
the fact
That friends are
rarely true
I really mean they
will not act
The way I want
them to.

TRUE LOVE

I don't pretend that
life's all good,
That Nature's always
sweet and kind.
I love the world
the way it is—
The truest love is
never blind.

TRUE SUCCESS

A true success my
life can be
Though fame and riches
I renounce.
It isn't what life
gives to me
It's what I bring
to life that
counts.

TRUE VALUES

Wealth of purse or
wealth of heart—
I know which one I'd
choose.
The things of truest
worth in life
Are those we cannot
lose.

TRUTH

Truth is the holy
grail I seek,
Beyond all small
ambitions.
The only truth I've
found is this—
Truth changes
with
conditions.

TUNING-UP

I heard musicians
tuning up,
And thought, "The
discord and the strife
That seem to fill my
days right now
Are just the tuning-up
for life."

TWILIGHT

Twilight is the lovely
time
When light and darkness
meet
As joy and sorrow
often touch
In one mood
strange
and sweet.

TWO LIVES

Because time goes
too fast for me
I can't do half the
things I ought —
I have two lives,
the one I act
And one I only live
in thought.

UNAFRAID

Life can't scare me
any more.
Out of woe is courage
born.
"Is this the worst that
you can do?"
I say to Fate,
and laugh
with scorn.

UNCHANGING

Although I might earn
wealth and fame
And win a high and
honored place
I can't achieve my one
great aim—
I'll have to keep
the same
old face.

UNDERNEATH

On top my thoughts
are nice and neat
With noble words and
manners sweet,
But when some crisis
stirs my mind
I'm just
surprised
at what
I find!

UNDERSTANDING

Sometimes our friends
may seem quite false
But we should still try
not to lose them—
If we could see within
their minds
It might be easy to
excuse them.

UNINVITED

Although I hate
receptions
I'm not at all delighted
To hear the mayor
gave one
And I was not
invited.

UNIQUE

Although I grow from
the human race
As a twig from the
parent tree
I never can think of
myself that way
But as wholly
uniquely me.

UNREPENTANT

I used to be quite
 foolish
When I was young
 and gay,
And though I'm now
 much older
I'm glad I'm
 still that
 way.

UNSELFISHNESS

Unselfish people share
 the joys
Of everyone they
 know —
We shouldn't need
 this argument
To be unselfish
 though.

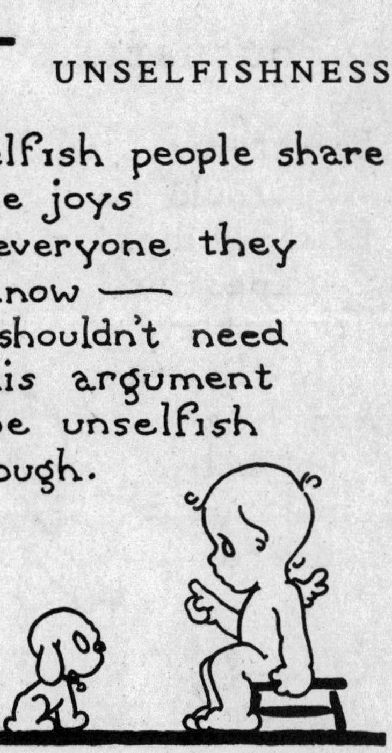

UNSHARED JOY

The place for sorrow
is solitude
Alone it is better to
bear it —
But the loneliest thing
is to find a joy
And not be able to
share it.

UNTOUCHABLE

Sometimes I wish that
I could be
Like ladies in a
tapestry,
To turn my profile
to the race
And live
untouched
in languid
grace.

UP AND DOWN

The water flows now
high, now low,
While forging onward
with a will.
Thus life should have
now joy, now woe—
For only
stagnant pools
are still.

UPLIFT

I've dramatized my
life too much
I'm so poetically
gifted.
At concerts I don't
listen now—
I sit and try to look
uplifted.

VACATION

My work just worried
me today
So that I couldn't do
my best
Until I had this lovely
thought:
The world can stand
it if I rest.

VALUE OF WORK

It's true you have to
work to live
For if you haven't
work to do
You can't impress
yourself on life
And then life hardly
touches you.

VALUES

I love my cat and yet,
alas,
He wants to eat my
pet canaries.
What different aims
we have in life—
I and my strange
contemporaries.

VANITATUM

When I gaze in the
looking glass lately, alas,
It's not my own face
that I see—
That I must grow older
like everyone else
Seems just too
surprising
to me.

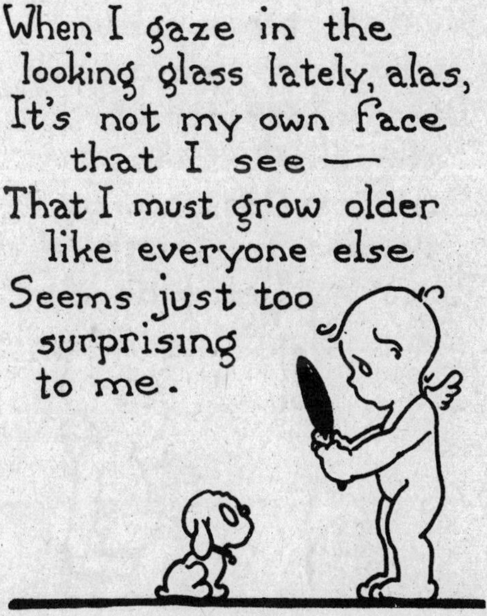

VANITY

The things in life I
 really want
Are all quite moderate
 and wise —
The foolish things I
 think I want
Are just to dazzle
 others' eyes.

VERBOSITY

We talk too much —
 why must we speak
Our unconsidered
 thoughts aloud?
Such careless words
 reveal no truth —
They rather hide it
 in a cloud.

VERY HUMAN

The bees go humming
 about their work
Like fat old women—
 I think they're funny—
They grumble away about
 practical things
And complain of the very
 poor grade
 of honey.

VICTORY

No one is a victor in
 life,
Whatever short triumph
 is his,
Unless in his heart he
 has made
His peace with
 the world
 as it is.

VIEW

If its windows hold
 a view
The smallest room
 seems unconfined.
So, if my thoughts
 range far and wide
No narrowness
 can cramp
 my mind.

VIEWPOINT

No other two people
 can ever have
Such different points
 of view
As the man who sub-
lets a furnished flat
And the tenant
 he rents
 it to.

VIEWS

Other people's lives
look strange to me.
I often wonder what
they're all about.
The only view of any
life that's clear,
I think, is from
the inside
looking out.

VIOLETS

The violet's shy but
it's obvious why:
The hiker just sees her
to seize her.
Let's let her alone by
her famed mossy stone.
I'm sure that such
treatment
would please
her.

I've worked to build
my character.
I wish I'd not
commenced it,
For virtue is its
own reward—
That's what
I have
against it.

VISTAS

Life spreads out
entrancingly
In vistas strange
and hazy—
They'll never be
more clear to me
Because my mind
is lazy.

VITAMINES

How joyfully I used
to eat!
No more such rapture
o'er me steals—
Now vitamines and
calories
Compose my spare and
studied meals.

VOCABULARY

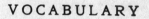

Cross word puzzles
broaden one
Although they're far
from easy sledding—
Who ever thought of
Ra before
Or knew that hay
was dried
by tedding?

VOICELESS

Though words have filled
my mind with music,
Made my lonely hours
gay,
When I want them, at
receptions,
Silently they
flit away.

WAITER

I love to find a waiter
kind
Who hides the haughty
way he feels
And treats me like an
equal, till
I quite enjoy my
humble meals.

WAITING

At times it's best to
  sit quite still,
Let go my stubborn
  little will,
And calmly, trustingly
  await
With unconcern my
  certain fate.

WALL

Selfishness is like a
  wall,
A useless wall, without
  a doubt —
It cannot hold my
  own joy in
But only keeps the
  world's joy out.

WANDERLUST

The railroad train with
plumes of smoke,
The ship with trails
of foam,
The road with winding
curves, in spring
All beckon
me from
home.

WASTE

I've wasted many
precious days,
A thought that fills
me with distress—
Stretched end to end
they'd make a line
To reach from
here to bright
success.

WASTED DAYS

This growing old has
brought to me
A sense of guilt that
always lingers—
I feel my wasted
days in crowds
All point at me
accusing
fingers.

WATER

How strange water is—
it can roar in the sea
Or tinkle fine songs in
a dell.
It washes our clothes and
makes nice cups of tea
And is lovely
to swim in
as well.

WATERFALL

One time I climbed
a mountain tall
And stood beneath a
waterfall
Of icy water blue
and clear —
I wish I had that
mountain here.

WATER STARS

Gay breezes dance
across the lake
And kick up waves with
quick light heels.
Great stars shine down
at night and make
Small water stars for
fish and eels.

WEAKNESS

Life was given me to
use,
But when it makes
me tired or blue
I'm letting it use *me*
instead—
And that's a foolish
thing to do.

WEALTH

I used to long for
worldly wealth
But though I'm
penniless today
I find since I've
revalued life
I'm really wealthy
anyway.

WEARINESS

I feel so weary in the
spring.
I long for nothing
but to rest.
It's lucky I am not
a bird —
I'd never build
myself
a nest.

WEATHER

I love grey days of
wind and rain
When all the big trees
shout and play,
And misty days all
filled with dreams—
I just love
weather
anyway.

WEAVER

I take a star, the
scent of rain,
A bird song light as
bubbles —
With these I weave
a shining veil
And cover up
my troubles.

WHAT OF IT?

Every word we say is
said forever.
Our smallest deed
can never be undone.
A solemn thought, yet
after all, what of it?—
There's no use
letting that
spoil all
our fun!

The noonday whistles'
piercing shrieks
To me are music
wild and sweet—
With gladsome cries
that reach the skies
They tell the world
it's time
to eat.

WHITE LIE

I'm always honest
with my friends
And look them squarely
in the eye—
And yet, alas, I
cannot say
I've never told
myself
a lie.

WHITHER?

?

"Whither are we drifting?
Indignant writers say,
But they ought to give us credit
For drifting quite a way.

WHY?

Whene'er I'm in revolving doors
Behind a fat and pompous man
Why am I moved to spin around
As fast and furious as I can?

WICKED DEEDS

When men are brave
or strong or good
I feel a pride in
what they do—
And when I hear of
wicked deeds
I feel I'm somehow
guilty too!

WILFUL

I make new mistakes
every hour
As down my life's
pathway I waltz,
But I won't have just
negative virtues—
I'd rather have
positive
faults.

WINDOWS

The whole world looks
a dreary place
When through soiled
windows it is seen.
A lesson this should be
to us
To keep our
mental
windows
clean.

WINGS

Hear the fine, endless
song of the fly
Who skims on his air-
colored wings —
Maybe stars as they
swing through the sky
Sing the same humming
song that
he sings.

WINTER

I like bad weather I
must admit.
I always have lived in
the midst of it.
I shout with the wind and
I roll in the snow—
I'll never grow up while
there's winter
I know.

WINTER CLOTHES

Time goes rushing
swiftly past me.
Far behind I slowly
drift.
Spring will come
before I know it—
Why then don
a winter
shift?

WINTER DAYS

The days in summer
  seem to me
To have more
  personality
Than winter days that
  quickly end,
Too cold to
  treat me
like a friend.

WISDOM

The wise old writers
  left advice
On how we might
  avoid life's stings.
To heed their words
  might cure our woes—
Except they all said
  different
  things.

WISH

I want all kinds of
feelings in my life.
We gain from all our
joys and sufferings.
Contentment gives us
health and beauty too,
And courage is the gift
that sorrow
brings.

WIT

I think of witty
things to say.
I'd be considered
bright —
Except I always
think them in
The middle of the
night!

WOE

I find that woe is
never quite
As final as I feared.
Thus as I flounder
through my life
I feel a little
cheered.

WORDS

Words have colors
and music
And wisdom and joy
as well —
How lovely I think
that words are
There are no words
to tell!

WORD SLAVE

Of yore my life was
carefree
And never sad or
grave —
But now these cross
word puzzles
Have made me just
a slave.

WORK

I'm glad I have to
work to live —
I'd hate to reach my
final day
And have a guilty
feeling then
That I had
never paid
my way.

WORLDS

We make each one our
separate world
Of all we do and
see,
And as I learn and
grow I feel
My whole
world grow
with me.

WORLD UNTOUCHED

In youth I was all for
reforming the world,
But now I've more
tolerant grown
I seem to prefer it the
way that it is—
I'm glad that I
let it alone!

WORRIES

Little worries swarm
like gnats
And cloud the
brightest day —
And yet the wind of
common sense
Could sweep them
all away.

WORSHIP

In my mind there
dwells a hero,
Brave and wise and
fair to see —
No one in the world
would know him
Or could guess that
he is me.

WORST FOE

Once you have
conquered your fear
You can face all the
world undismayed
For fear is an enemy
worse
Than the danger
that made
you afraid.

WRINKLES

My mind has held a
million thoughts.
They pass and seem
to leave no trace—
Yet by degrees, as
years go by,
They write a story
on my face.

X-RAY

We congregate in
stylish groups
And smile and chatter
at a tea—
If we could see each
other's thoughts
What consternation
there would be!

YAWNS

I'm yawning from
morning till night.
It's awful the hours
I keep—
I simply can't live
long enough,
I'm afraid, to catch up
on my sleep.

YEARNING

When people yearn
with all their hearts
For just one treasure
far away
They close their eyes
to countless joys
That crowd
around them
every day.

YOUNGER SELF

Looking back I dimly
see
A younger self who
lonely stands.
His face is turned
away from me.
He reaches out
his empty
hands.

YOUNG EYES

This world is really
very old.
Its outlines rarely
change —
And yet to each new
pair of eyes
It looks both
new and
strange.

YOUTH

Youth brings the
greatest gladness,
Or so I'm often
told —
And I can always
keep it
Unless my heart
grows old.